HOW TO Motivate Reluctant Learners

ROBYN R. JACKSON

Alexandria, Virginia USA

mindsteps
Washington, DC

1703 N. Beauregard St. • Alexandria, VA 22311-1714 USA
Phone: 800-933-2723 or 703-578-9600 • Fax: 703-575-5400
Website: www.ascd.org • E-mail: member@ascd.org
Author guidelines: www.ascd.org/write

mindsteps™
Washington, DC
Phone: 888-565-8881
Website: www.mindstepsinc.com

Gene R. Carter, *Executive Director;* Judy Zimny, *Chief Program Development Officer;* Nancy Modrak, *Publisher;* Scott Willis, *Director, Book Acquisitions & Development;* Genny Ostertag, *Acquisitions Editor;* Julie Houtz, *Director, Book Editing & Production;* Katie Martin, *Editor;* Reece Quiñones, *Senior Graphic Designer;* Mike Kalyan, *Production Manager;* Circle Graphics, *Typesetter*

PAPERBACK ISBN: 978-1-4166-1092-2 ASCD product #110076 n5/11

Quantity discounts for the paperback edition only: 10–49 copies, 10%; 50+ copies, 15%; for 1,000 or more copies, call 800-933-2723, ext. 5634, or 703-575-5634. For desk copies: member@ascd.org.

Library of Congress Cataloging-in-Publication Data

Jackson, Robyn Renee.
How to motivate reluctant learners / Robyn R. Jackson.
p. cm. – (Mastering the principles of great teaching series)
Includes bibliographical references.
ISBN 978-1-4166-1092-2 (pbk. : alk. paper)
1. Motivation in education. 2. Effective teaching. I. Title.
LB1065.J24 2011
370.15'4–dc22

2011013403

20 19 18 17 16 15 14 13 12 11 1 2 3 4 5 6 7 8 9 10 11 12

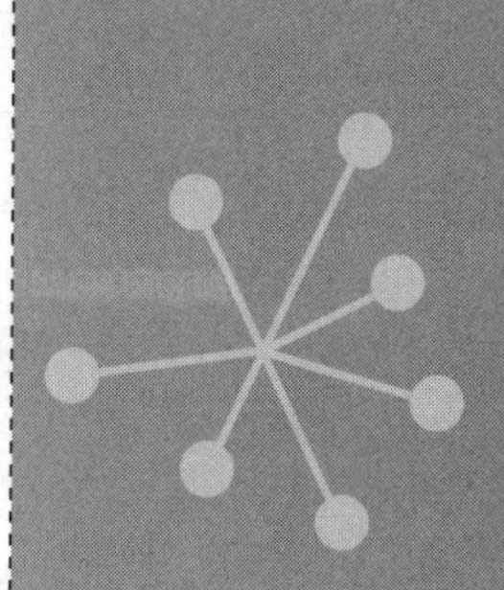

MASTERING
THE PRINCIPLES OF GREAT
TEACHING

How to Motivate Reluctant Learners

About the Mastering the Principles of Great Teaching Series 1

How to Use This Guide 4

Self-Assessment: Starting Where Your Students Are 9

Introduction: Understanding the Mastery Principle 13
What we call "motivation" in school is really a decision students make to invest their currencies in our classrooms.

1. **Identifying the Right Investments** 21
How do you motivate students to invest in your classroom? The first step is to determine what specific investments you want them to make.

2. **Creating a Classroom Worth Investing In** 36
You have identified and refined the investments you want students to make, but have you considered the ways in which your classroom practices and procedures might be standing in your students' way? Your next task is to set up a classroom environment that is conducive to investment.

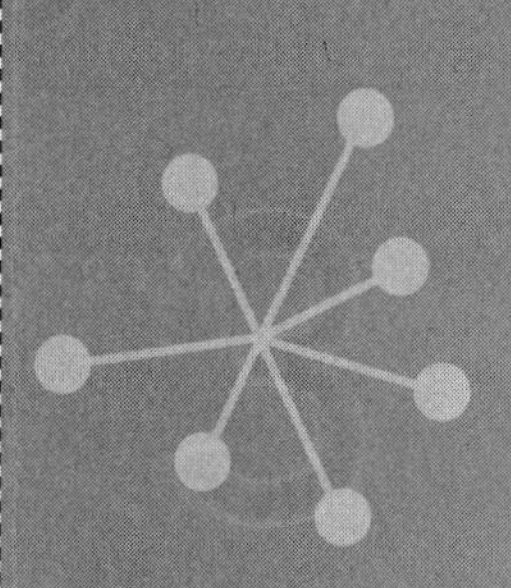

About the Mastering the Principles of Great Teaching Series

Have you ever wondered what it takes to become a master teacher? Sure, you know what master teachers do—what their classrooms look like, how they structure their lessons, the kinds of assessments they give, and the strategies they use. But becoming a master teacher involves more than simply doing what master teachers do. To be a master teacher, you need to *think* like a master teacher.

If you ask master teachers their secret, they may not be able to tell you. That's because most master teachers have a difficult time explaining what makes them masterful in the classroom. Much of what they do in the classroom feels automatic, fluid, and natural. To them, their mastery is simply *teaching*.

How did they get so good? How did they become master teachers, and how can you become one yourself? The answer is that master teachers have learned how to rigorously apply a few simple principles of great teaching to their practice. They have, in short, developed a master teacher mindset.

The seven principles of mastery teaching are

1. Start where your students are.
2. Know where your students are going.
3. Expect to get your students to their goal.
4. Support your students along the way.
5. Use feedback to help you and your students get better.
6. Focus on quality rather than quantity.
7. Never work harder than your students.

As you can see, none of these principles is particularly earth shattering. They are things we all know intuitively that we should be doing in the classroom. But the master teacher mindset develops as a result of systematically and rigorously applying these principles to teaching until they become our spontaneous response to our students. The more you practice these principles, the more you too can begin to think like a master teacher, and the closer you will come to having a master teacher mindset.

How can you start to practice these principles in your own classroom? How can you do so in a way that is true to your own style and suits the learning needs of your particular students? How, in other words, can you systematically apply mastery principles to address the everyday challenges you face as a teacher? This series will show you what to do.

If you discovered this series through its companion book, *Never Work Harder Than Your Students and Other Principles of Great Teaching* (Jackson, 2009), you'll find some familiar concepts covered here. While *Never Work Harder Than Your Students* introduced the principles of mastery teaching, the how-to guides in the Mastering the Principles of Great Teaching series will take you step-by-step through the process of integrating those principles into your classroom practice and show you how to apply the principles to resolve specific teaching challenges you face.

Each of the how-to guides in this series focuses on one of the seven mastery principles. You'll examine the principle, assess your current practice of the principle, and learn new ways to incorporate it in your teaching. And because the series is designed to show the mastery principles in relation to specific teaching challenges, working your way through each guide will help you to resolve many of your immediate, day-to-day classroom challenges even as you build your overall mastery mindset.

Mastery teaching is not about fitting into a specific mold, and these guides are designed to help you grow no matter where you are in your practice. If you have read *Never Work Harder Than Your Students,* you may recall that it includes a diagnostic tool to help teachers assess their skill level in each principle and locate themselves along a mastery teaching continuum ranging from novice to apprentice to practitioner to master teacher. Each of the how-to guides in this series also begins with a diagnostic tool to help you identify where you fall on the continuum so that you can focus specifically on the strategies best suited to your current practice. This format ensures that you will be able to work through all the guides at your own pace and level, cycle back through, and, with each rereading, deepen your understanding and further the development of your master teacher mindset.

The guides in the Mastering the Principles of Great Teaching series follow a standard format. After an introduction to the focus mastery principle and the diagnostic, you will work through chapters that prompt you to apply the principle rigorously and systematically to your classroom practice. Along the way, you will learn new strategies, develop new skills, and take time to reflect on your growth. The tools in each guide help you take a close look at your own teaching, examine your assumptions about teaching and how students learn, and refine your instruction so that your students can learn more effectively.

Becoming a master teacher has little to do with how many years you put in or how closely you resemble a particular Hollywood ideal. It isn't some special gift doled out at birth to only a chosen few. Any teacher can become a master teacher with the right kind of practice—the kind of practice this series of how-to guides offers. In working through them, you too can develop a master teacher mindset and be the master teacher your students deserve.

How to Use This Guide

At the heart of most theories and books on motivation is a presumption of effort—the idea that even students who are disengaged or disruptive will put forth some effort or comply with classroom rules most of the time. Teachers know how to handle students who are occasionally disengaged. We all also have some idea of how to handle disruptive behaviors so that students will comply with our rules even if they are not wholeheartedly cooperating. And we can work with kids who are at least willing to go through the motions. But what about students who have opted out entirely? What about students who openly resist our best efforts? While many motivational theories work well for students who are willing to at least play the game of school, they often don't address what to do about students who do not even try and may even be out-and-out hostile to learning.

This how-to guide shows you how master teachers motivate the most reluctant students—the ones who actively fight efforts to help them learn or passive-aggressively resist attempts to engage them. Rather than review tricks and strategies for setting up reward systems, or present creative new ways to entice or cajole students to do their work, this how-to guide will help you develop a plan for getting students to choose to invest in their own learning and engage meaningfully in the classroom.

The key is to examine motivation from a different perspective. We'll start by thinking of students' knowledge, effort, abilities, and interests as "currencies"—things of value that they can "invest" in order to obtain something they want: additional knowledge or skill, satisfaction, validation, status, and so on. Through this lens, motivation can be seen as the decision students make each day to invest those currencies in the classroom. Based on the mastery principle "Start Where Your Students Are," this guide shows you how to determine what investments you need students to make in your classroom, shape your classroom to make it more likely that students will make those investments, identify and address the reasons students aren't investing in your classroom, and invite students to invest in your classroom and sustain their investment over time.

Use this guide to read, reflect, plan, and implement strategies that will make your classroom a place where all your students are actively participating in their own learning. Regardless of the grade level or discipline you teach, the concepts and strategies in this book will help you help your reluctant students discover their competence, successfully navigate school culture, take risks in the classroom, and become engaged in their learning.

How This Guide Is Structured

How to Motivate Reluctant Learners begins with an **Introduction to the Mastery Principle** and a **Self-Assessment**—a diagnostic tool to help you identify where your current application of the principle "Start Where Your Students Are" falls on the continuum of mastery teaching. Then, it's on to the guide's five chapters, each helping you take another step toward developing a comprehensive approach to motivation:

- **Chapter 1: Identifying the Right Investments** will help you figure out what motivation looks like in your classroom. You'll reflect on the skills and behaviors you value most and determine the specific investments you want students to make in your classroom.
- **Chapter 2: Creating a Classroom Worth Investing In** will help you uncover and remove any practice- and procedure-related barriers that may be unintentionally demotivating your students. You'll learn about the unique needs and expectations of 21st-century learners and ways to use autonomy, mastery, purpose, and belonging to create a classroom climate that students will find worth their investment.
- **Chapter 3: Understanding and Addressing Student Resistance** focuses on uncovering the reasons students are unmotivated and shares ways to start overcoming

their reluctance to learn. You'll learn how to help students let go of defensive stances and "I don't care" attitudes and begin to use their powers for good.

- **Chapter 4: Asking For and Shaping an Investment** offers ideas for how to ask for the right investment in the right way. You will learn how to use "the five Be's" to secure students' initial commitment to invest in your classroom and how to steer them toward successful engagement.
- **Chapter 5: Putting It All Together** shows you how take all that you have learned throughout this guide and develop a plan for helping students shift from unmotivated to motivated behaviors in the classroom. You'll also learn strategies for sustaining their motivation over time.

Throughout the guide, **Your Turn** sections provide suggestions for how to begin taking action in your own classroom. These suggestions are divided into four levels, keyed to your current level of principle application:

- ***Acquire.*** The suggestions here are designed to help those working at the novice level develop a better understanding of the principle and of their own teaching practice as it relates to the principle.
- ***Apply.*** The suggestions here focus on showing those working at the apprentice level how to use the guide's strategies in their teaching practice.
- ***Assimilate.*** The suggestions here are designed give those working at the practitioner level additional ideas about how to incorporate the principle and strategies into their existing practice.
- ***Adapt.*** The suggestions here will help those working at the master teacher level take a fresh look at their own practice and customize some of the guide's strategies in a way that's right for them and their students.

Think of this guide like a spiral staircase in which you return to the same concepts more than once, each time pushing yourself to an incrementally higher level as you proceed toward mastery. The breaks between each level are natural "rest stops"—places where you will know you've made substantial progress and can pause so that you won't feel overwhelmed or stuck before moving forward. Rest assured, even if you don't move beyond the *Acquire* suggestions your first time through the guide, you will still have made progress. Stop there and try those skills out in your classroom. Then, as your ability and confidence grow, you can return with the next unit in mind.

Each time you will continue enhancing your practice by ramping up to the apprentice level and beyond as you build your master teacher mindset and refine your practice.

Tools

Within each section, you'll also find other tools to help you reach your goals, including

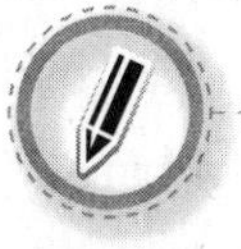

Checklists outlining what you will accomplish at each step.

Time-Saving Tips to steer you toward information that will allow you to complete each step more quickly.

Checkpoint Summaries that quickly summarize some of the main concepts in this guide. You can use these to assess your own understanding of specific concepts and as a handy reminder of some of the key points.

Take It Step by Step boxes that summarize the key steps in a process and serve as handy reminders later on.

Learn More Online sections that point you to other strategies and additional resources available on the web.

Think About sections that raise reflection questions designed to prompt you to consider what you've read and make connections to your own classroom and teaching practice.

Yes, But . . . sections addressing common objections and reservations teachers sometimes express in relation to these strategies. These sections will help you resolve some practical challenges and overcome any hesitation you might be feeling.

You will also find a variety of worksheets, planning templates, and strategy sheets that will help you capture your learning and build a comprehensive plan. The **Appendixes** at the end of the guide offer a reference list of student currencies, a selection of instructional strategies designed to address the root causes of student resistance, and an example of a complete motivation plan. Feel free to write in this guide, make copies of the worksheets, or download resources on the companion website, www.mindstepsinc.com/motivation.

Your Approach

If you are working through this how-to guide individually, first take time to understand the book's general framework. Preview the material and make a commitment to spend a certain amount of time each week working through the various steps. You can read through the book entirely before deciding where to begin, or you can jump right in and start trying some of the strategies outlined. Either way, be sure to reflect periodically on how applying these strategies affects your practice and your students. Then, adjust your practice accordingly.

If you are working through this book with other teachers in a small-group setting, begin with an overview of the various steps in the process and discuss which steps might give each group member the most trouble and in which steps members of your group might have some expertise. Use this information to designate a group facilitator for each step in order to keep everyone focused and on track. Then, make a commitment as a group about how you will work through the steps individually, and meet regularly to discuss your progress, share your triumphs, and brainstorm ways around your challenges. You can use the "Think About" sections as a starting point for group discussion and then share individual strategies that you have implemented in the classroom.

If you are an administrator or teacher leader, this book will give you an overview of the planning for motivation that should be happening in every classroom. And it will provide you with useful tools you can offer to teachers as you conference with them and support their professional development.

Share Your Progress

As always, we want to hear from you! Contact us at info@mindstepsinc.com to ask questions, share your experiences, and pass along success stories of how you've motivated your students. Administrators and district-level leaders are welcome to contact us to learn more about the supports Mindsteps Inc. offers for teachers and schools; give us a call at 1-888-565-8881, e-mail us at info@mindstepsinc.com, or visit us on the web at www.mindstepsinc.com.

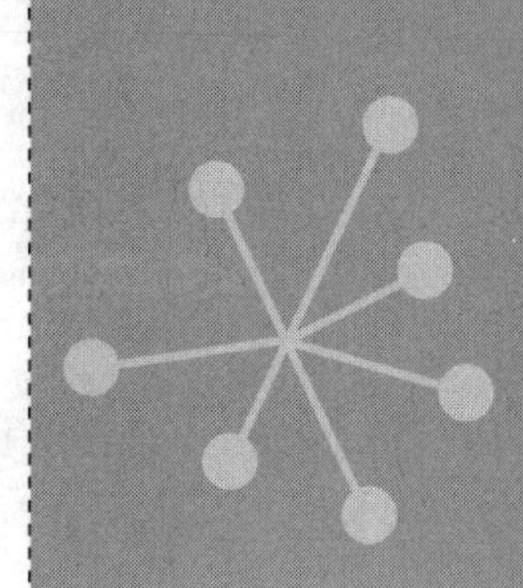

Self-Assessment: Starting Where Your Students Are

Answer each of the following questions as honestly as you can; don't think about what you would like to do but about what you currently do in your own practice. There are no right or wrong answers.

1. The following statement best captures my general thoughts on motivation:
   a. I believe that students should come to school intrinsically motivated to learn.
   b. I believe that students can develop motivation over time.
   c. I believe that students need to be inspired in order to be motivated.
   d. I believe that students will be motivated if they enjoy the work they are asked to do and have fun activities.

2. When I am faced with a resistant learner, the first thing I do is
   a. Look for a solution.
   b. Try a variety of solutions to see which one works best.
   c. Think about what may be causing the problem, and select a solution that fits the situation.
   d. Look for patterns, and develop a solution that will address not only the surface problem but also the underlying causes the pattern reveals.

3. When it comes to teaching "soft skills," such as study habits and organization skills, I
    a. Expect my students to know how to do those things already. It is not my job to teach them how to be good students.
    b. First look at how students naturally use their soft skills, and then show them how to improve what they are already doing so that it is more effective.
    c. Require that my students use specific soft skills and conduct checks to make sure that they are doing things the way that I ask.
    d. Show my students various ways to develop their soft skills, then let them choose how they will use their soft skills in the classroom.

4. When my students come to class without the "soft skills" that they need to be successful, I
    a. Try to teach students the skills they need even if it means that I don't always get through my entire curriculum.
    b. Look for ways to help students acquire those skills that are most necessary while trying to get through as much of my curriculum as I can.
    c. Look for ways I can show students how to capitalize on the skills that they do have in order to acquire the skills that they don't have.
    d. Talk to the students' counselors to make sure that they are properly placed in my class.

5. When a student is reluctant to participate in my class, I
    a. Question whether the student is academically capable.
    b. Question whether the student is motivated.
    c. Question whether I have failed to consider alternate ways that the student might demonstrate mastery or motivation.
    d. Question what I can do to get the student to meet my class expectations.

6. When it comes to rewarding my students, I
    a. Try to find rewards that I think will motivate them to keep up the good work.
    b. Decide on a reward system in advance and provide these rewards as students meet specific criteria.
    c. Pay attention to what students value and find a way to connect what they value to what they should be doing in the classroom.
    d. Abstain. I don't typically reward students. Learning is reward enough.

From *Never Work Harder Than Your Students and Other Principles of Great Teaching* by R. R. Jackson, 2009. Alexandria, VA: ASCD. Copyright 2009 by Robyn R. Jackson. Adapted with permission.

7. The following statement best captures my practices concerning classroom structure:
   a. I tweak my classroom structure each year based on the feedback I get from my students.
   b. I completely alter my classroom structure each year so that it can capitalize on my students' backgrounds, experiences, and preferences.
   c. I don't change my basic classroom structure from year to year, but I do try to make it easier for students to adjust to my structure.
   d. I don't change my basic classroom structure. I feel that students need to learn to adjust to a variety of classroom structures and rules because it helps them prepare for college and the real world.

8. I see a resistance to learning as *primarily*
   a. A values problem.
   b. An emotional problem.
   c. A discipline problem.
   d. An academic problem.

Scoring

For each question, circle the number in the column that represents your answer. For instance, if you answered B for question 1, you would circle the 2. When you have finished, calculate the total for each column and determine your grand total by adding up the four column totals.

Question	A	B	C	D	
1	1	2	3	4	
2	1	2	3	4	
3	1	4	2	3	
4	2	3	4	1	
5	1	2	4	3	
6	1	2	4	3	
7	4	1	3	2	
8	4	1	2	3	**Grand Total**
Total					

Going Forward

Use your grand total to determine your of current level of principle application and locate the most appropriate suggestions for taking action in your own classroom.

8–11 points: Novice

If you scored in the novice range, focus on the ***Acquire*** suggestions. If some of the ideas and practices discussed are familiar, you may wish to jump to the suggestions under the *Apply, Assimilate,* and *Adapt* headings. As you build your confidence with the *Acquire* actions, return to this book and work through it again at a different level.

12–19 points: Apprentice

If you scored in the apprentice range, focus on the ***Apply*** sections. Try some of the ideas and approaches in this guide and pay attention to how they work for your students and to what feels right to you. As you become more comfortable applying these ideas, or if you are already implementing some of the practices in the *Apply* sections, consider the *Assimilate* or *Adapt* suggestions, and look for ways to refine what you are already doing.

20–27 points: Practitioner

If you scored in the practitioner range, focus on the ***Assimilate*** suggestions. Look for ways to begin integrating more of this guide's recommended approaches into your overall practice so that your use of them becomes more automatic and comprehensive. If a particular practice is new to you, start at the *Acquire* or *Apply* suggestions and work your way up to those under *Assimilate.* If a practice is embedded into your teaching habits already, try some suggestions associated with the *Adapt* heading.

28–32 points: Master Teacher

If you scored in the master teacher range, focus on the ***Adapt*** suggestions. Many of the approaches presented in this guide are already a part of your classroom philosophy and practice. Your goal should be to customize the *Adapt* suggestions to your students and your classroom context. If you come across an idea that is new to you, take time to work through the *Acquire, Adapt,* and *Assimilate* suggestions so that it too can become a seamless part of your overall practice.

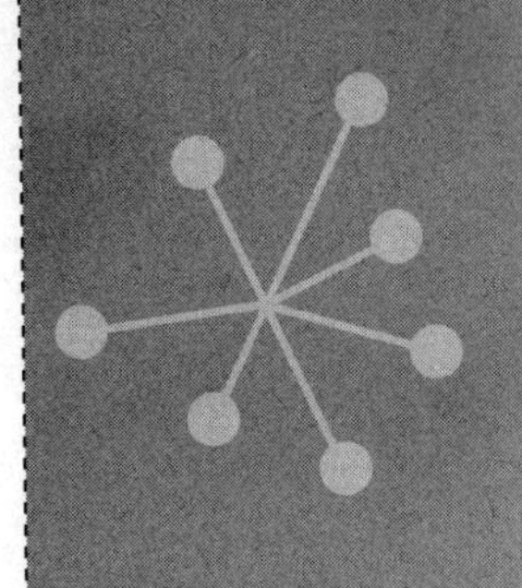

Introduction: Understanding the Mastery Principle

What we call "motivation" in school is really a decision students make to invest their currencies in our classrooms.

All of us have a portfolio of knowledge and skills we've accumulated through our various experiences. We might know the difference between a nine-iron and a driver and when to use each because we golf every weekend with our buddies. We might know how to cook a perfect roast chicken because our grandmother showed us the secret. We might be able to explain the latest developments in the financial markets or in Congress because we follow the news. We might be the life of the party because we have collected an array of funny jokes and anecdotes over the years.

What we know and can do makes us the people we are and also functions as a form of currency in various aspects of life. Knowing the difference between a nine-iron and a driver, for example, "buys" you social and athletic status among your golfing buddies. It makes you look like you know what you are doing, helps you play a better game of golf, and ensures that you won't make a laughable mistake when it's your turn to tee up. Knowing how to cook that perfect chicken "buys" you the envy of your friends, high praise from your family, and the satisfaction of good food done well. Keeping up with the latest news "buys" you small talk with your colleagues in the teachers' lounge or with your fellow commuters on the train. Being the life of the party "buys" you a constant stream of invitations and the admiration of others.

We all use what we know and can do to navigate our worlds and to form and maintain relationships. And we rely on these currencies to acquire *new* knowledge and skills and access new experiences. The same is true for the students in our classrooms. If they know the vocabulary that we are using to explain a new concept, they can follow our lesson. If they know how to take excellent notes and have effective study habits, the odds are that they will earn high marks on the challenging unit test next week. If they are able to control their impulses and follow the class rules, they can get through the school year with a clean behavioral record and maybe even earn our favor.

In the context of the classroom, there are four primary forms of currency:

- ***Knowledge:*** Typically this is the type of currency valued most in schools. Students are measured by what they know, and what students know gives them access to other knowledge and a greater understanding of concepts. But the kind of knowledge that functions as currency extends beyond that which is explicitly taught to include background knowledge and general cultural literacy that we sometimes wrongly assume all our students will have.
- ***Soft skills:*** This type of currency includes the skills students use to access classroom content and navigate the school culture, such as study skills, organizational skills, and time management. If students don't have these soft skills, they have a much harder time learning and interacting in the classroom.
- ***Social skills:*** Learning is socially mediated; we learn from, through, and with others. Knowing how to forge and maintain relationships allows students to feel connected, provides a sense of belonging, and gives them access to others who can help them learn. Social skills involve, first, knowing how to read a social situation, and second, knowing what to say, to whom to say it, when to say it, and how to say it so that we get what we want from the situation. Students who lack these kinds of currencies may have a difficult time attaining goals.
- ***Network affiliations:*** In a knowledge-based economy, who you know can perhaps be even more important than what you know, because through these connections you gain access to more experts and more knowledge bases. The communities and social groups to which students belong also shape their priorities and give them information on how to behave in various situations.

Appendix A provides a list of general currencies grouped in these four categories. It's important to stress, though, that these are just a subset of the vast depository of currencies any individual student might possess. All our students' knowledge, skills, and behaviors—their interests, abilities, experiences, preferences, talents, and everything else that makes them who they are—have different values in different dimensions of their life: at home, with friends, on the basketball court, in the dance studio, at the skateboard park, in online gaming circles, in social media settings, at church, and so on. The challenge for us is to design lessons, use instructional strategies, and create a classroom climate in which everyone's currencies, teachers' and students', are valued and can "buy" a desirable end.

Currency and Motivation

Cognitive scientists argue that all behavior is purposeful. We do something because doing it will get us something that we want. And so, for example, we might go to work every day because it garners us a paycheck, we enjoy socializing with colleagues, we derive satisfaction from helping students learn, and myriad other reasons. Our students might turn in their homework because they want a grade, they want to meet our expectations (or their parents'), they enjoy learning, they believe that the homework will help them develop a set of skills they desire, and so on. Our students might act out in class because they want attention, they want to exert control over the classroom, they want to release frustration and tension, they want to get kicked out so that they can hang out in the principal's office, or any of a number of reasons. All behavior, "good" or "bad," is purposeful.

For students, the choice to "invest" in a classroom is also purposeful, and students who do so expect a return on that investment. They may study because they believe that doing so will help them earn an *A*. They may pay attention because they've learned that doing so will earn them the approval of their teacher. They may complete the reading assignment because they are interested in the topic and enjoy reading about it.

Our students' decision to invest in the classroom is directly related to whether or not they have the currency our assignments, activities, and broader academic and behavioral expectations are asking for—and whether or not they believe that currency will help them achieve a desired outcome or meet a particular need. While this decision is not always conscious, it is indeed a decision that is every student's to make. It determines whether they will attempt difficult work or sit passively by, whether they will persevere through frustration or give up, whether they will participate in the classroom culture or reject it, and whether they will embrace challenge or avoid it.

This decision is the source of most motivation issues in the classroom. Every day, currency is exchanged and negotiated in the classroom. When we teachers can demonstrate the value of what we have to offer (e.g., additional knowledge and skills, good grades, approval, engagement, recognition, a new perspective), students will choose to invest in our classroom. If it happens that they do not possess the particular currency an assignment or classroom expectation requires, these students will be willing to do the work to acquire it, because the appeal of what that knowledge, skill, or behavior can "buy" will be so strong. But when students do not see the value in what we are offering, they won't invest, even if they have the currencies to do so.

CHECKPOINT SUMMARY

Classroom Currencies

Include knowledge, soft skills, social skills, and network affiliations.
Exchangeable for something desired (e.g., information, status).
Negotiated and traded among teachers and students.
Help students acquire new knowledge, skills, relationships, and experiences.

"Unmotivated" Students

In truth, it's a misnomer to call a student "unmotivated." All human beings have drives and engage in goal-directed behavior. "Unmotivated" students are not without drives. They are not unmotivated 24 hours a day, 7 days a week; they are simply not motivated by what they find in school. It's not that they don't invest themselves in anything; it's that they have decided not to invest themselves in your classroom.

Imagine that you are at a party and someone tells a joke. Everyone but you laughs raucously. They all get it; you don't. How do you feel? What goes through your head? What do you do? Do you laugh along anyway so that you aren't left out? Do you stand there with a baffled look on your face, mumbling "I don't get it"? Do you pull a friend aside later to get her to explain the joke? Do you worry that everyone will think you are an idiot for not getting the joke?

Now imagine what some of our students must feel like in the classroom when everyone else seems to be getting it. How must they feel when they see other students successfully navigating the classroom when they don't have the required knowledge or skills and are at a loss for what to do? It can feel like everyone is in on the joke—everyone but them. Typically, they will try to hide fact that they don't understand, pretending to get it or simply withdrawing from the situation in various ways, be it sitting in silence, not completing assignments, not turning in homework, or not showing up for the test. As a result, we may see them as "lazy" or unmotivated. These students may have tons of other currencies in their metaphorical pockets—just not the currencies we're asking for. They logically assume there is there is no place for them in the classroom "marketplace," and so they simply opt out.

Perhaps more tragically, sometimes students *do* have the specific knowledge, skills, and experiences we want them to invest in our classroom but choose not to invest them. They get the joke, but they refuse to laugh (if they've shown up for the party at all). These students may sit in the back of the room and ignore the assignments completely, or they may do things to disrupt the learning of others. Either way, they have decided that although they have the currencies they need to learn, they'd rather invest those currencies somewhere else.

Reasons for this kind of resistance vary, but often it comes down to value. These students don't see the value in what we are trying to teach them or the way that we want them to invest (e.g., completing assignments, engaging in class discussions, studying, paying attention). And unless we address their objections and demonstrate the value of the ends and the means, they will repeatedly resist investing in our classrooms.

Start Where Your Students Are

All of this talk about currencies, investing, and value are really just ways to help you start where your students are. If you can understand what currencies your students carry and value, and then help them invest those currencies in the classroom, you can overcome even your most intractable motivation issue.

Starting where your students are means that you are willing to get to know your students on more than a superficial level, because being able to start where your students are implies *knowing* where they are—why they aren't currently investing in your classroom and what would make such an investment valuable to them. If we are going to help *every* student achieve success—even the boy who currently spends the entire class period with his head down on his desk, or the girl who shrugs in response to every question posed to her—we need to get a feeling for what they need and value. What kinds of currency are they carrying? On what would they be willing to "spend" their currencies? What do they find valuable? This understanding is a starting point for helping them choose to invest in our classrooms.

The typical response to students who decide not to invest in the classroom is to try to make what we are doing in the classroom more engaging. We work hard to inspire them and cajole them. We create games or competitions or "fun" projects. We show movies and take them to really "cool" websites. We scour the library for a funny book or litter our worksheets with clip art to make them more "visually interesting."

Other times, often with noble motives, we attempt to compel students to do what we ask. After all, we make kids eat their vegetables and enforce bedtimes because it is good for them. Shouldn't we do the same when it comes to their academics, forcing them to do their work or come to extra study sessions because this, too, is good for them? No, not if we really want to motivate them. You see, there is a difference between motivation and control. Control is making someone do what you want them to do; motivation is helping someone *choose* to do what you ask them to do. See the difference? Motivation isn't about compliance or control; it's about choice. Rather than look for ways to compel or trick students into doing what we ask (and liking it!), we can help them make the choice to invest their currencies in the classroom.

This isn't easy. Because motivation is based on a range of factors, no single approach will work all the time and with every kid. So if you are looking for a quick fix to help you get your students to do what you want them to do when you want them to do it, you won't find it here. What you *will* find is a different way of looking at motivation and your students. You will learn strategies for building the kind of classroom culture and environment that invites even your most resistant learners to invest in your classroom. And you will also explore ways to make learning feel so safe and look so attractive that all students will want to lower their resistance, shed their armor, and take the risk to learn in your classroom.

THINK ABOUT . . .

Take a moment to reflect and write down a few notes. Who are your unmotivated students this year? What have you done to try to reach them?

YOUR TURN

Acquire: Think about your own students. Make a list of the investments you want them to make in your classroom this year.

Apply: What investments have you asked your students to make in your classroom? Make a list of the currencies these investments require.

Assimilate: Over the next week, observe your students. When do they choose to invest in your classroom and when do they opt out? What currencies are they willing to invest, and what currencies do they choose not to invest? What reasons can you discover for their investing or choosing not to invest?

Adapt: Divide a piece of paper into two columns. On one side, list the currencies your students carry. On the other side, list the currencies demanded by your classroom. Now, examine both lists. What are the similarities? Where is there a mismatch? How might the similarities help students invest in your classroom? What can you do to mitigate the mismatches so that more students can and will invest in your classroom?

YES, BUT . . .

What about MY currencies?

Recognizing and honoring students' currencies doesn't mean that you must abandon your own preferences. The key is to look for ways to find common ground. Maybe you prefer lecturing, but your students aren't good note-takers. Provide them with a note-taking sheet that can help them take better notes, and stop your lecture periodically to allow them to compare their notes with yours or with a partner's. Perhaps you prefer a quiet classroom, but your students want to talk as they work.

Set aside quiet time for them to work individually, and then give them time to interact with their classmates. Or take them to the computer lab and allow them to work together in chat rooms you set up. That way, the class is still quiet, but the students have multiple opportunities to interact. This is not an either/or proposition. You can find ways to honor your currencies while also honoring your students'.

Fundamental Assumptions

In this guide, I make some assumptions. First, I am assuming that you have something valuable to offer students and that you have planned engaging lessons and have a challenging curriculum. If you do not, it may not be that your students are unmotivated—they may simply be bored. For help on planning engaging, challenging, and rigorous lessons, check out the *How to Plan Rigorous Instruction* guide in this series. I am also assuming that you have set up supports to make sure that your students can access challenging instruction. If you haven't, your students' disengagement may be more about frustration than a lack of motivation. For help on building appropriate support structures into your instruction, see the *How to Support Struggling Students* guide in this series.

1

Identifying the Right Investments

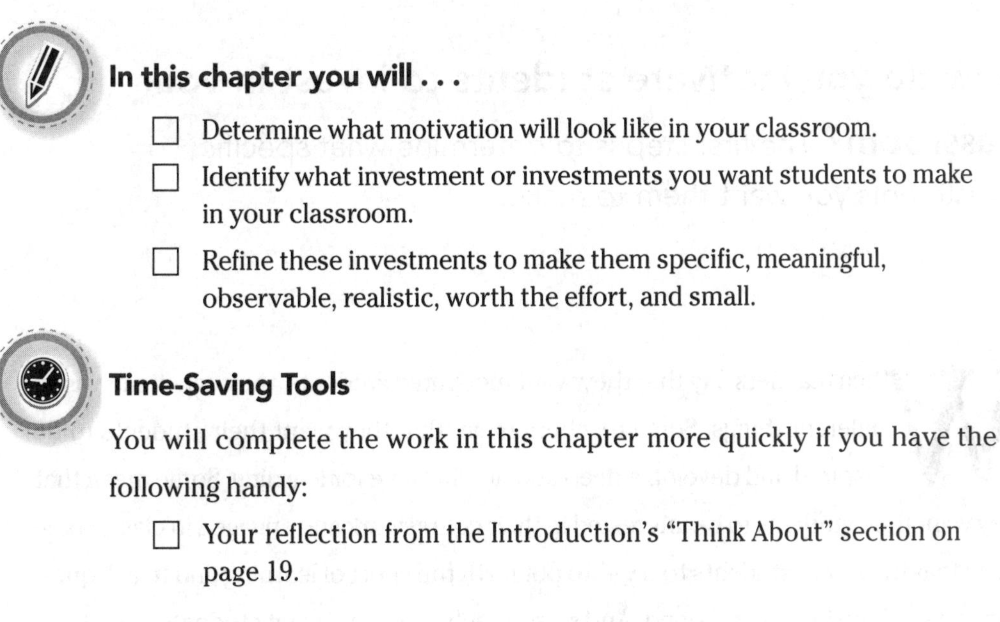

In this chapter you will . . .

- ☐ Determine what motivation will look like in your classroom.
- ☐ Identify what investment or investments you want students to make in your classroom.
- ☐ Refine these investments to make them specific, meaningful, observable, realistic, worth the effort, and small.

Time-Saving Tools

You will complete the work in this chapter more quickly if you have the following handy:

- ☐ Your reflection from the Introduction's "Think About" section on page 19.

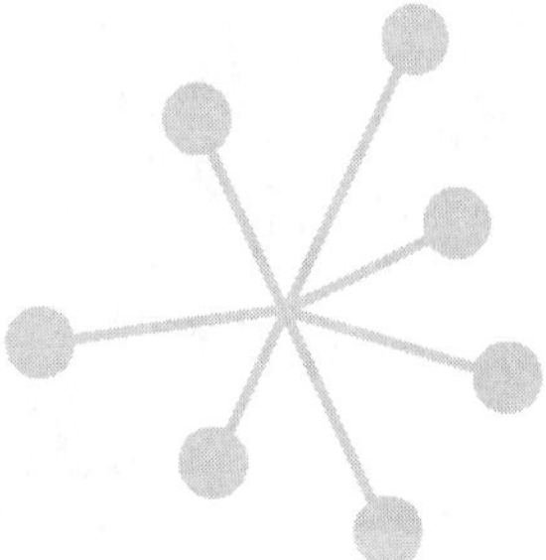

How do you motivate students to invest in your classroom? The first step is to determine what specific investments you want them to make.

When teachers say that they want motivated students, they can mean vastly different things. Some teachers mean that they want their students to be inspired and develop a deep and abiding love for learning. Some mean that they want their students to be interested in their coursework and engaged in class. Some mean that they want students to try— to put forth the effort of learning and to ask questions when they don't understand. And some teachers simply want students to do their homework and come to school on time. These are all different kinds of investments.

Further complicating things is that our ideas about the kinds of investments we want students to make may or may not be realistic, or even important. We may want them to wriggle with excitement every time we pull out the place-value mats, or smile with delight each time we pass out another Elizabethan sonnet to discuss, but are excitement and delight actually prerequisites to learning? We may want them to keep meticulous desks or carefully catalog every handout using a more complicated version of the Dewey decimal system, but can students still learn effectively when their desks are less than spotless and their notebooks less than pristine? Before we work on how to get students to invest in our classrooms, the first step is to make sure that we are asking for the right investments.

What Does Motivation Look Like to You?

Often when I ask teachers what motivation would look like in their classrooms, they say, "I just want them to care." But when I push further, they have a hard time telling me what "caring" would look like. Motivation can be an ambiguous goal. If we are going to help our students become more motivated, we have to first translate that ambiguous goal into concrete behaviors.

So when you say that you want your students to be motivated, what do you mean? How would they behave? What would they feel? How would they react to new learning? Take a few minutes to think through what motivation looks like to you, using the questionnaire on pages 24–25 to guide your reflection.

Reflections on Motivation

1. How do unmotivated students currently behave in your classroom? What do they do (or not do)?

2. How do you think these unmotivated behaviors affect students' individual ability to learn and the classroom environment as a whole?

3. Imagine that a miracle occurred, and that you walked into class one day to find that all of your students' motivation problems had been solved. Describe what this would look like over the course of a typical class. What would your students be doing differently?

4. Take a closer look at the "miraculously motivated" class you've described above. What specific investments of time, effort, and attention do you envision students making?

5. How do you think the specific investments you've identified would affect your classroom environment?

6. How might you respond to students differently if they were suddenly motivated? What specific behavioral changes would they notice in you?

7. Describe the last time you saw your "unmotivated" students invest in your class even for a little bit of time.

8. Look closer at this motivated episode and consider what about it might have been different. What was different about the activity, the classroom environment, and your behavior that might have motivated your "unmotivated" students to invest in your class?

THINK ABOUT . . .

Based on your answers to the questionnaire, what investments in your classroom seem to be the most important to you? Why do you think you value these behaviors so much?

YOUR TURN

Acquire: Study your students over the next few weeks. List all the ways that they are currently investing in your classroom using the currencies you're asking them to use. Pay attention to when they invest and then think about the times that they choose not to invest. What is the difference? What seems to be influencing their investment choices?

Apply: List three specific investments you want your students to make in your classroom (you can use the questionnaire to help you). Then pay attention to which students are currently making those investments and which are not. Why do you think they are making the choices they are making? What supports might your students need in order to invest in the way that you desire?

Assimilate: Think about all the ways you help your students invest in your classroom. What supports do you use, and what structures are already in place to help your students invest in the ways that are important to you? Identify what other supports and structures you need to add to help *all* your students invest consistently in the ways that you have identified.

Adapt: Think about investing from your students' perspective. What investments are they currently asking from you? Study their behavior over the next two weeks, and identify the investments (e.g., time, attention, supports) your students may be waiting for you to make in them before they will invest in your classroom.

The Right Kind of Investment

Now that you have thought through the investments you would like your students to make in the classroom, the next step is to determine whether those investments are really the right ones for your students. For instance, you may want your reluctant students to start doing their homework every night, but is that the best place to start? Would they be better off in the long run if they made a different investment instead?

It is important to identify the right investments up front so that you don't waste time trying to get students to do things that don't really matter to their learning or success. Identifying the right kind of investment will also help you focus students' attention and energy in the right direction. This is especially true for students caught in a cycle of failure who may be downright resistant to making any investment at all.

Your students are more likely to invest in the classroom if what you ask of them is *Specific, Meaningful, Observable, Realistic,* worth the *Effort,* and *Small.* The acronym SMORES can help you remember these criteria.

Criterion #1: Specific

Often students don't invest in our classrooms not because they don't want to but because they don't know how. What looks like resistance can simply be confusion. Thus, it is important that any investment we ask them to make is clear in terms of the behaviors we're asking for and the component parts of those behaviors. So instead of making vague requests ("OK, will you try harder to complete your homework next time?"), ask students to agree to do something very specific ("Will you commit to completing a minimum of nine problems on your next assignment?"). Instead of telling them to "pay attention in class" or "arrive ready to learn," clarify what each investment requires: keeping their head off the desks, keeping their eyes open and on you, being in their seats with their materials out at the bell, and so on. This degree of specificity lets students know what is expected of them and gives them concrete steps for making the investment.

Another reason specificity is important is that our idea of motivated behavior may be vastly different from our students' idea of motivated behavior, and they may manifest their motivation in ways we may miss. Perhaps your students do care about their learning and success but don't show their caring in a way that you can recognize. Perhaps your students are investing but are not using the particular currencies you have in mind. While you are looking in vain for students to demonstrate engagement through active, vocal participation in discussions, they may be demonstrating engagement by listening carefully and silently processing the discussion. Making your investment requests specific provides clarity to everyone, and allows you to put structures in place to facilitate the investment and monitor students' success.

Criterion #2: Meaningful

We often think that if our students just *understood* how important it was for them to do their homework each night or why missing class puts them at such a disadvantage, they would change their "unmotivated" ways. So we set off to explain our reasoning. But it isn't that students don't understand the importance of coming to class or doing their work; it's that understanding isn't enough. Unless we identify an investment we want that is meaningful to them, they will not choose to invest.

Two quick questions can help you determine whether the investment you have in mind will be meaningful in students' eyes:

1. *Does it provide students with a way to use the currencies they have to get something they want?* The investment should involve them using something they know and can do to accomplish a goal, acquire new and useful currencies, or solve an interesting problem.
2. *Does it provide students with a way to use their currencies to satisfy a need?* The investment should involve them using something they know or can do to meet a need for safety and survival, connection and belonging, power and competence, freedom and autonomy, play, enjoyment, or fun (Maslow,1943).

If you can answer "yes" to one of these questions, the investment you have in mind is one that students will find meaningful and will thus be more likely to make.

Criterion #3: Observable

We may want students *to care, to try, to want to learn,* but take a moment to think about what these three often-hoped-for investments have in common. They are all emotions. The only way that we know that students do care, are trying, or want to learn is by their behaviors. If we don't couch the investment we want students to make in terms of observable behaviors, then we open the door to frustrating subjectivity.

For instance, suppose you want students to try harder. What does *trying harder* look like? How will you be able to tell whether your students are trying harder? And how will you be able to hold students accountable for making an investment when you have no tangible way of knowing that they are trying other than their saying so?

Imagine if you instead asked students for an investment that is observable: doing all of their work according to set requirements for completion and quality, attempting to answer questions even when they are unsure if their answers are right, asking for help when they don't understand, and going back over their work and fixing errors that have been identified. Conceiving of and expressing the investments you desire as observable behaviors gives students a clearer picture of what you want. And it gives you a solid way of determining whether or not students have the currencies they need to make the investment, a better way of demonstrating to them the value in the investment, and a better way of monitoring students' investment over the days and weeks ahead.

Criterion #4: Realistic

Most teachers agree on the merits of having high expectations, but pushing students to do something that's beyond their achievable limits is more likely to damage motivation than build it. We tend to want unmotivated students to commit to changing everything at once, but that just won't work.

Instead, ask students to commit to doing something that feels doable to them. It cannot be a behavior so minor that the commitment itself seems silly ("Will you commit to at least putting your name on the paper?"), but it should not be so hard that the commitment seems overwhelming ("Will you commit to completing all assigned readings for the rest of the year and taking at least three pages of notes each time?").

One way to find an achievable investment is to pay attention to what the students are investing in already and then select an investment that is similar but perhaps one step beyond and achievable with supports. For example, if you have students who come to class but are late every day, start by asking them to commit to coming to class on time and give them strategies to do so. If you have students who are already doing the homework some of the time, ask that they complete the homework every night and provide them with supports, such as a template for writing down assignments and a way to access additional help if they get stuck. And if you have students who manage to focus on their work for just a few minutes at a time, ask them to increase these on-task behaviors, which will help them finish their classwork, and provide additional supports such as a quiet place to concentrate or strategies for breaking up an assignment into smaller parts with mini-breaks in between. The key is to start where students are and gradually help them move to where you want them to be.

Criterion #5: Worth the Effort

The purpose of getting students to invest in our classrooms is to advance their learning in some way. Asking them to complete assignments that are not very interesting and offer little value wastes both their time and yours. Asking a student to complete the work for the remainder of the semester at a point when it's become mathematically impossible for the student to pass will seem similarly pointless.

One way to make an investment worth the effort is to choose an investment with a short-term payoff. Short-term payoffs engender hope, which is really important for students who are reluctant to invest because of a history of failure. When students see how a small investment can lead to a big gain, it is evidence that success is within their reach.

Clearly, a good deal of making sure an investment is worthwhile depends not only on the type of behavior we're asking for but also on our own behavior. For example, you might want students to come to class on time and be in their seats when the bell rings, but this investment is only worth the effort for students if you are ready to start class promptly. Likewise, if you want students to work quietly and independently on their classwork rather than distract their neighbors with annoying behaviors, you must be sure to acknowledge when they *do* work quietly and independently rather than distract their neighbors. For reluctant learners, motivated behavior that goes unacknowledged may not seem worth continued effort.

Criterion #6: Small

For many students, investing in the classroom in the way that we would like them to invest can be really tough. Our digitally minded, 21st-century learners may struggle, for example, with an expectation that they will sit quietly and read from the textbook or a novel for long stretches of time. And for students with a history of failure, requests for big changes in behavior will seem particularly daunting. Although they may want to do better in school, they often don't have a clear sense of what "doing better" even means—let alone how to go about it.

Motivated behavior can seem like a big change for students; the trick is to find ways to make it small and doable. A student may not be able to commit to caring every day for the rest of the year but probably can commit to completing a single week's worth of homework. Chip and Dan Heath (2010) call this incremental approach "shrinking the change." In their book *Switch: How to Change Things When Change Is Hard,* they argue that "one way to motivate action is to make people feel closer to the finish line than they might have thought" (p. 127).

Motivation is never one big shift; it's the result of several smaller shifts in a student's thinking and effort. Over time, these small shifts lead to big changes. So rather than focus on asking students for BIG investments at first, find a small change they can make—a tweak to their behavior that sets them on the pathway to a bigger investment. Instead of asking a chronically tardy student to come to class on time, perhaps you ask him to beat the time he came to class today by 30 seconds. If he's able to continue doing this over the course of a few days, he'll soon be getting to class on time. Rather than asking a student to complete the entire project, break the project down into baby steps. I once got a very resistant group of 11th graders to complete a 10-page research paper by telling them that we were going to write five two-page papers. Once they turned in all the two-page papers, we spent a class period writing transition paragraphs to connect them into a single 10-page paper.

Asking for a small investment seems counterintuitive, I know. But shrinking the change is a powerful way of helping resistant and reluctant learners make an initial investment. The first step is the hardest, so it makes sense to make it a small step. Once students realize that they can make progress from a small investment, they may be motivated to keep it up and eventually make bigger investments.

CHECKPOINT SUMMARY

The SMORES Criteria for Shaping the Right Kind of Investment	
Specific	The investment should consist of specific steps rather than a vague request.
Meaningful	The investment should help students use the currencies they have to get something they want or meet a basic need.
Observable	The investment should be stated in terms of its observable behaviors.
Realistic	The investment should be at the top of students' "reach" given their present currencies.
Worth the **E**ffort	The investment should lead to immediate and short-term payoffs.
Small	The investment behavior should not be something students will perceive as overwhelming.

THINK ABOUT . . .

Which of the SMORES criteria seems to be the hardest for you to apply to the investments you want your students to make in your classroom? Why do you think this is?

YOUR TURN

Acquire: Think about the current investments you are asking your students to make in your classroom. Use the SMORES criteria to refine these investments to make it more likely that your students will choose to make these investments in your classroom.

Apply: Think about the investments your students are making already. Then use the SMORES criteria to select one additional investment you would like your students to make in the classroom.

Assimilate: Think about the investments you are asking your students to make already. Using the SMORES criteria, identify what additional supports you could provide to make those investments more likely and consistent.

Adapt: Pay attention to the investments your students are making already. Identify which of the SMORES criteria seems to be most significant in your students' choices to invest in your classroom. Based on your observation, prioritize the SMORES criteria to better fit the needs of your students, and use this prioritized list as a starting point for selecting or shaping additional investments you will ask of your students.

Focusing on the Investments You Want

Now, try your hand at refining one of the desirable investments you identified on page 26 by completing the **Investment Analysis Worksheet** on pages 33–34.

Investment Analysis Worksheet

Target Investment: What is one key investment you want students to make in your classroom?	
Specific: What specific actions do you want students to take in order to invest in your classroom?	
Meaningful: How will this investment help students use their currencies to meet their basic needs?	
Observable: How will you know that students are making this investment? What observable things will you see and hear from them?	

(continued)

Investment Analysis Worksheet (cont.)

Realistic: Is this investment achievable given students' current abilities and currencies? How so?	
Worth the **Effort:** What immediate and short-term payoffs will students receive as a result of this investment?	
Small: How can you shrink the change so that students' initial investment feels doable? What "baby steps" can you help students make toward this investment?	

YES, BUT . . .

Won't these criteria look different from student to student?

They will. Many important investments we want students to make in the classroom may not immediately fit the SMORES model for every student. For instance, completing homework may be a small step for some students and a mammoth step for others. Or what may be meaningful to one student may seem positively banal to another. That's OK. The point of the SMORES criteria is not to come up with a one-size-fits-most investment to ask for from your students but to help you think through any investment you are asking students to make and consider how to make that investment more accessible. Sometimes you will be able to settle on something that appeals to all of your students. Other times, you will need to refine your approach to meet the different needs of several students or groups of students. While this may seem like a lot of work, consider it an investment on your part. By thinking through, tailoring, and refining the investments you are asking of your students up front—even if it means adjusting that investment to meet the different needs of various students—you save yourself time and a lot of frustration in the long run.

2

Creating a Classroom Worth Investing In

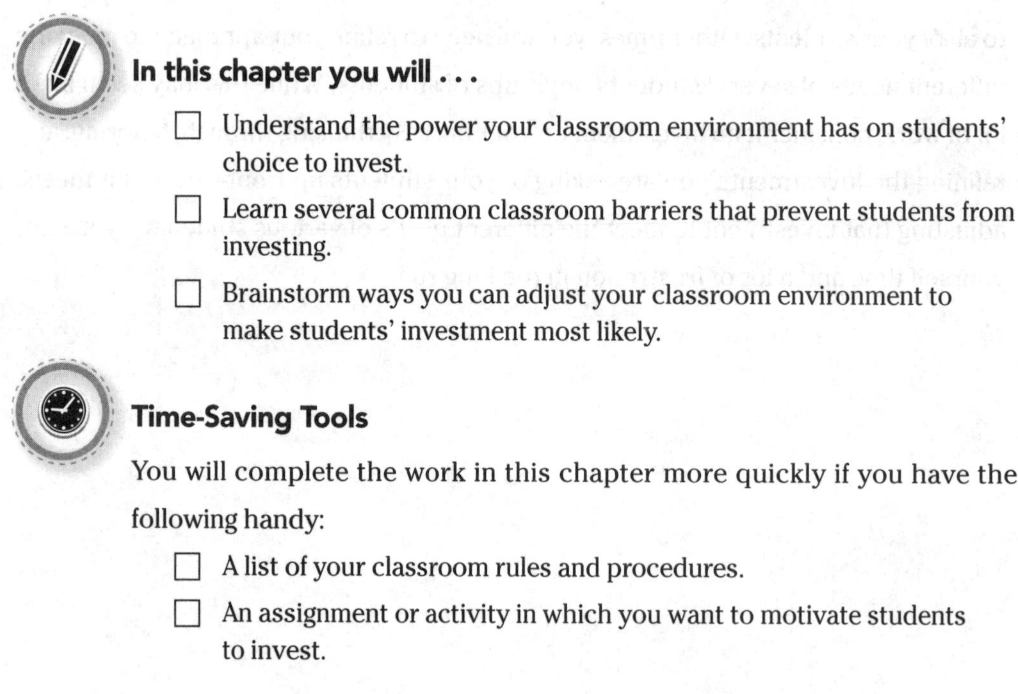

In this chapter you will . . .

- ☐ Understand the power your classroom environment has on students' choice to invest.
- ☐ Learn several common classroom barriers that prevent students from investing.
- ☐ Brainstorm ways you can adjust your classroom environment to make students' investment most likely.

Time-Saving Tools

You will complete the work in this chapter more quickly if you have the following handy:

- ☐ A list of your classroom rules and procedures.
- ☐ An assignment or activity in which you want to motivate students to invest.

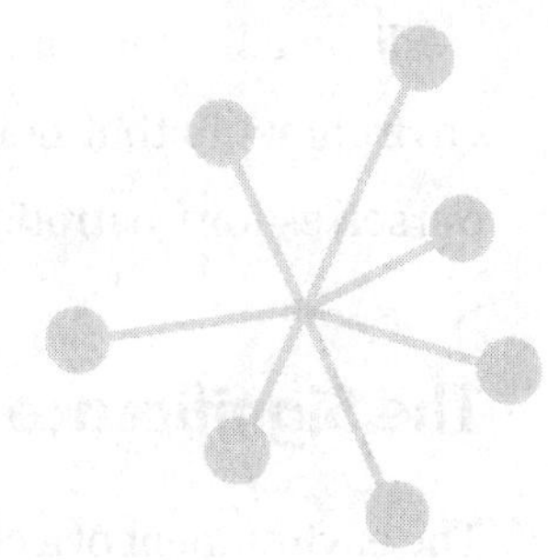

You have identified and refined the investments you want students to make, but have you considered the ways in which your classroom practices and procedures might be standing in your students' way?

Your next task is to set up a classroom environment that is conducive to investment.

We spend a lot of time lamenting a lack of student motivation. We point to uninvolved parents or video games or laziness or outside distractions in the community as causal factors. But we may be missing a huge deterrent to motivation sitting right under our noses and entirely within our control—our classrooms.

Our classrooms often present unintentional barriers to learning that can actually undermine student motivation. For instance, perhaps we want students to engage in productive group discussion but have not established the guidelines or interpersonal scaffolding they need to be successful. Or perhaps we want our students to stop cutting class but have not made any special efforts to engage students in learning when they do show up. Maybe we ask them to be independent thinkers and learners but have not planned rigorous learning experiences that will build their capacity for rigorous thinking over time. Maybe we ask them to honor our currencies—to love history as we do or to work quietly and alone, as we prefer to work—while barely recognizing their currencies.

If we ask students to invest in our classrooms without also creating classroom environments that help them invest successfully, we set up both our students and ourselves for frustration.

The Significance of Classroom Climate

The environment of a classroom affects behavior in subtle ways. Think of how students transition more smoothly from one activity to the next when they have a routine in place to do so. They usually complete their assignments more easily when they have clear directions, and they tend to work better in groups when there are clear norms for group work. The opposite is also true. A disorganized classroom tends to decrease time on task, and poor or muddled directions often result in work that's incomplete or completed incorrectly. Absent clear classroom rules, students can't be sure what behavior is acceptable and what is not.

In this chapter, we are going to look at ways we may be unintentionally making it difficult for our students to invest in our classrooms. This will involve starting where our students are and considering our classrooms from their perspective. We will examine a few common classroom barriers to investing and look at ways we can tweak our classroom environments to make investing easier.

20th-Century Classrooms, 21st-Century Students

The problem of motivation is magnified when 21st-century learners are asked to navigate 20th-century classrooms. In 20th-century classrooms, learning was essentially linear. Problems had logical solutions, and there were usually step-by-step processes for arriving at an answer. Because learning was linear, so was motivation. Teachers tended to employ a standard series of rewards and punishments. If students complied, they received rewards; if they failed to comply, they faced punishment. The expectation was that if students did what they were told, they would be successful.

But the kind of learning necessary in the 21st century is not so much linear as it is geometric. We face complex problems, and new technologies and the ubiquity and speed of information mean that arriving at the answer is no longer a strictly step-by-step process. To solve problems, we juggle multiple perspectives and navigate a complex maze of data. And in a nonlinear world, where students no longer necessarily expect *A* to lead to *B,* motivation efforts based on a system of rewards and punishments no longer work. There are plenty of rewards to be found outside school, and many traditional punishments have lost their sting. Suspension no longer excludes students from learning or from their social circles. They can chat with their friends throughout the day and keep up with everything that is going on in the classroom without having to bother actually attending. They might even find a more interesting and engaging learning experience online. Detention or staying in at recess is easily endured when it's possible to text or play games on a cell phone.

Our students may seem unmotivated in the classroom, but outside the classroom they devote hours to building new websites, updating their blogs and social networking profiles, texting friends, reading material online, and mastering complex video games. The learning they do on their own is dynamic, multimodal, mobile, and collaborative. Traditional classroom activities—controlled, one-way, static, and meant to be done alone—offer few chances for students to use the skills and knowledge they see as valuable.

If we want to motivate 21st-century learners, we first need to find ways to make our classrooms more conducive to their 21st-century currencies. Happily, it's possible to do this by making some simple shifts in instructional practice. For instance, instead of always having students complete assignments independently, include more opportunities for collaboration. Rather than rely on the textbook as the sole source of information, allow students to learn through a variety of media, such as film, websites, and podcasts. Instead of having students solve problems with predictable solutions, give them problems with unpredictable outcomes and real-world applications. (For more on how to do this, see the *How to Plan Rigorous Instruction* guide in this series.)

Second, instead of trying to move our 21st-century students toward the behaviors we'd like to see via carrots and sticks, we need to step back and allow them to take these steps on their own. The task here is to identify and remove barriers to investment and set up a classroom that students will choose to take part in.

20th-Century Learning	21st-Century Learning
Single-tasking	Multitasking
Linear	Geometric
Independent	Collaborative
Individually owned	Shared
Stationary	Mobile
Deductive	Inductive
Achieved through hard work	Achieved through leverage
Focused on the What	Focused on the Why
Text-based	Multimedia-based
Physical	Virtual
Local	Global
Mechanized	Creative
Other-directed	Self-directed
Predictable	Unpredictable

THINK ABOUT . . .

Examine your classroom through the lens of a 21st-century learner. In what ways is your classroom conducive to 21st-century learning, and in what ways is it not? What shifts could you make in your instructional practices to bring in more aspects of 21st-century learning?

Classroom Barriers to Investing

Our students come to us with a myriad of experiences. Some of those experiences prepare them to do well in school, while others seriously impair their ability to invest in their learning.

Many of these factors teachers cannot control. We cannot control the kinds of parents our students have. We cannot control the amount of sleep they get each night. We cannot control their nutrition or their home study environments. We cannot control how much money their family has or how that money is spent. We cannot control what our students do outside school, who they play or hang out with, or where they go and what they see as a result. While all of these things can significantly affect students' motivation, they are outside teachers' control. What we can control—in fact, the *only* thing we can control—is what we do in the classroom.

Let's focus on what a teacher *can* do to remove three common classroom barriers that prevent students from investing. As you read, think about your own classroom and the investments you want your students to make. Look for ways that you might be unintentionally preventing students from investing successfully in your classroom.

Classroom Barrier #1: Requiring Currencies Students Don't Have

I once coached a teacher who told me about taking his students to the computer lab to create tables to illustrate data they'd gathered during a science experiment. After 20 minutes in the lab, none of the students had completed their tables. He reminded the students that the tables were due at the end of the period, and he moved from student to student, encouraging them to get their tables done. He even threatened the distracted students with detention if they didn't get back on task. But these efforts didn't do much good. At the end of the period, nobody had completed the assignment.

Initially, the teacher bemoaned his students' lack of motivation. It seemed to him that they just couldn't care less about graphing their data. What he realized after the fact was that his students simply didn't understand how to use the spreadsheet program. It wasn't that they didn't want to do the work or were choosing to surf the web or chat with their friends instead; they just didn't have the currencies that the assignment required.

This was a case of a teacher unintentionally creating a classroom barrier to student investment, and it happens all the time when we give assignments with directions that are unclear or that ask students to apply currencies they do not possess. The way to figure out if this barrier is a factor in your classroom is to examine each assignment and activity during the planning stage and identify exactly what it's asking students to do. What currencies—what tools, skills, and knowledge—will students need to complete the assignment or participate in the activity? Do all your students have access to these tools? Do all your students know how to use these tools? Do they all have the skills and knowledge that the assignment or activity is asking them to apply?

Classroom Barrier #2: Not Clarifying Which Currencies Are Required

You may know very well which skills, knowledge, and behaviors each of your assignments and activities is calling for, but it's a mistake to assume that your students always do.

During planning, take a look at your assignments and the associated materials. Look for ways you can make requirements clearer. For example, will students need to look up vocabulary words in a dictionary in order to complete the assignment? Is this point noted in the assignment's directions? Does a full mark for participation in a class discussion require students to look at the person who is speaking? Could you remind students of this requirement before the discussion starts and throughout the conversation? Will students need to complete the assignment in a particular way? Would it help to provide and explain a sample response or performance before they begin their work?

After focusing specifically on which currencies your students will need to complete an assignment, take a little more time to figure out how you can communicate that understanding to them.

Classroom Barrier #3: Insisting on Our Preferred Currencies

Most of us are not fully aware of the currencies we value in the classroom—or the influence this valuation has on our instructional decisions and classroom policies. The truth is a teacher's preferred currencies have a powerful effect on students' motivation. Clearly, if students have the currencies they need to be successful in the classroom, they are more likely to invest in what's going on. However, if we insist on students always using the specific set of currencies we value most without giving them a chance to use any of the other currencies they bring with them, we limit their opportunities for investment and even risk shutting some of them out entirely.

Identifying this third classroom barrier to investment involves taking a careful look at your instructional decisions and classroom rules and policies. Ask yourself whether you might be unintentionally demotivating students by insisting on your way and your way only. For example, you may prefer that students write only in ink, but is it really necessary to require them to do so? You may believe it's valuable for students to complete an anticipation guide and fill in a note-taking template every time they read a textbook chapter for homework, but is doing so really indispensible to learning? You may think that the best kind of group discussion are those in which each individual takes a turn speaking and there is no cross-talk or interrupting, but is that how all your students would describe "the best kind of group discussion"?

Think about these preferred currencies that crop up in your instruction and ask yourself how essential these skills, ways of working, and ways of behaving really are to learning. For example, do students really need to keep their class notebooks according to your outline, or are there other organizational strategies that might also work? Do students have to sit in alphabetical order, or can they still get their work done and pay attention if they sit where they'd like?

In short, you can address this third classroom barrier by allowing students more options when it comes to tackling assignments, behaving, and demonstrating understanding. As noted, students are more likely to invest in a classroom where their ways of knowing, being, and doing are valued and accepted.

Analyzing and Removing Classroom Barriers

Before you can build a classroom worth investing in, you need to first identify and then remove classroom barriers to the investment or investments you want your students to make. I recommend a brainstorming approach based on the Haddon Matrix—a common analytical tool in the field of injury prevention—that will help you think systematically about classroom barriers to success. Your objective is to focus on three key time frames (what goes on before, during, and right after students invest in your classroom), identify potential impediments during each phase, and consider how these barriers could be addressed.

Imagine that a teacher wants his students to complete their homework each night. He makes homework worth a significant number of points, keeps students who haven't completed their homework after school and makes them do it then, and calls the parents of students who repeatedly do not complete their homework to enlist their help. None of these measures has had much effect. The **Sample Classroom Barrier Anticipation Worksheet** on page 44 illustrates how a Haddon Matrix–inspired framework can provide clarity on barriers to investment and help define the next steps in their removal.

Now you try it. Think about the target investment you selected in Chapter 1. Use the **Classroom Barrier Anticipation Worksheet** on page 45 to identify factors that may be keeping your students from making that investment, and brainstorm ways you might tweak your classroom environment to make it more conducive to investment.

Sample Classroom Barrier Anticipation Worksheet

Before the Investment	
What classroom barriers might prevent students from making the investment you're asking for? How can you remove these barriers?	• Unclear directions could be a problem. I usually ask students to read the homework assignments, but I don't tell them what to look for. Instead, I should give them a graphic organizer that helps them organize their notes on the chapter.
How can you make it easier for students to invest?	• Make the graphic organizer short—just one page long—so students feel like it isn't that much to complete. I could also give struggling students a graphic organizer that includes page numbers so they know where to look for the information.
During the Investment	
What classroom barriers might make it difficult for students to sustain investment?	• My reading assignments are pretty long—whole chapters. Students might get bored. • Some students are overcommitted (lots of challenging classes, after-school activities, jobs, responsibilities at home), and they might not have enough time to read the entire chapter.
How can you make it easier for students to sustain their investment?	• Create breaks in the chapter where students have to stop and complete part of the graphic organizer before they move on. • Tell students how much time it should take them so that they can plan for it.
After the Investment	
What classroom barriers might prevent students from repeating their investment?	• If my lecture tomorrow repeats the same information presented in the homework chapter, students might be less willing to complete homework reading; they'll see it as a waste of time. • If I don't ask them to use the information they got through the reading, they might feel like it was wasted effort and be less likely complete future homework reading.
What can you do to make students want to repeat their investment?	• Instead of lecturing on the chapter, I could have students use their graphic organizers to complete a class discussion or do some other fun group activity where they have to use what they learned the night before. That way, they will want to read the next time because they can see it as useful.

Classroom Barrier Anticipation Worksheet

Before the Investment	
What classroom barriers might prevent students from making the investment you're asking for? How can you remove these barriers?	
How can you make it easier for students to invest?	
During the Investment	
What classroom barriers might make it difficult for students to sustain investment?	
How can you make it easier for students to sustain their investment?	
After the Investment	
What classroom barriers might prevent students from repeating their investment?	
What can you do to make students want to repeat their investment?	

 This worksheet is available for download at www.mindstepsinc.com/motivation.

THINK ABOUT . . .

Examine your own classroom. What barriers could keep students from making the target investment you identified in Chapter 1's Investment Analysis Worksheet? How might you remove those barriers?

YOUR TURN

Acquire: Take a look at an upcoming assignment. Which, if any, of the three barriers to investment discussed on pages 41–43 are present in that assignment? How could you remove those barriers?

Apply: Spend the next two weeks observing your students and your classroom environment. Identify one or more examples of the barriers to investment discussed on pages 41–43, then develop a plan for removing those barriers.

Assimilate: Think about the strategies you have used already to remove barriers to learning in your classroom. Look for ways to apply these strategies to specific barriers to investment in your classroom.

Adapt: Think of additional barriers to investment beyond the three identified on pages 41–43 that might be present in your own classroom. Come up with ways to remove these barriers for students.

YES, BUT . . .

When you advise me stop insisting on my preferred currencies, are you saying my preferred currencies are "wrong"?

Teachers tend to teach according to the way that we ourselves learn best. This works out great for students who learn like we do, but it can be tough for students who don't share our learning style or preferences and have to adapt to our way of doing things, provided they have the currencies to do so.

It's natural to prefer particular sets of currencies, and you value these currencies for a reason. Often they're skills, knowledge, and behaviors that you know will support school success. Study skills, for example, are a preferred form of currency for most teachers simply because most of us have seen how students who study effectively are more likely to retain content, acquire and refine new skills, and ultimately understand key concepts. We're confident that students who carry and use this currency will have an easier time learning. What we must remember, though, is that study skills encompass a wide range of strategies. We get into trouble when we insist on students studying in one specific way rather than allowing them to choose from and experiment with a variety of study strategies and find an approach that is the most effective for them.

The key is to not allow your preferred currencies to overwhelm your classroom so that there are no spaces for students to use alternative forms of currencies to help them learn.

How to Build a Classroom Worth Investing In

The good news is that you can make your classroom more motivating by building in structures that make it easier for students to invest than to opt out. Researchers point out that motivation depends on a sense of autonomy, mastery, purpose, and belonging (Csikszentmihalyi, Abuhamdeh, & Nakamura, 2005; Pink, 2009). Making even small environmental tweaks to imbue your classroom with these qualities will make a huge difference.

Provide Students with More Autonomy

Let's start by acknowledging that you cannot give students complete autonomy. Not only do you have a curriculum to get through and standards to meet, but it's simply unfair to ask students to be their own teachers. What you can do is give students options that allow them to exercise some control over their own learning in certain areas. Pink (2009) suggests giving students more autonomy in four areas: *task, time, team,* and *technique.*

Build In Task-Related Autonomy

It's true that there are some specific tasks that all students must complete in order to master a particular objective, but where you have a little more wiggle room, allowing students to choose from several task options is much more motivating. Choice helps students create their own learning pathways and find their own ways of demonstrating their understanding.

You might create leveled learning contracts, use tic-tac-toe choice boards, or create tiered assignments. You might allow students to choose among several possible essay topics or choose a book from a list of several options. You might give students a choice about the format of their final project: give a speech, build a website, create a live model, or write a paper. The key is to make sure that the various task choices align with the learning goals and represent comparable levels of difficulty so that you don't unintentionally derail effort by offering an "easy" option.

To take it one step further, consider allowing students to decide on their task without giving them predefined choices. You might identify a percentage of your unit or class time where students are free to work on anything they want as long as they can demonstrate how this work will move them toward attainment of one or more of the clearly defined learning objectives you provide. Thus, you might run a writer's, reader's, or math workshop once per week where students independently pursue individual reading, writing, or math goals. Or you might allow students to design their own final projects within a set of parameters, design their own science experiments for a science fair, pick a research topic, conduct research, and hold a miniconference where they share their findings in any format they choose. In each case, students work within parameters to choose their own learning tasks.

By giving students some autonomy over the tasks they use to learn and demonstrate learning, you allow them to choose those tasks that are the best match for their preferred currencies. And, when students are allowed to capitalize on their currencies, they are often more engaged and more inclined to take ownership of their learning.

Build In Time-Related Autonomy

A lot of schoolwork is defined more by the amount of time students put into it than it is by the quality of the work and learning that may result. This is somewhat weird considering that there is very little correlation between how much time students spend on work and the quality of that work. Some students take hours to produce mediocre work, while others can zip off a perfect performance in a matter of minutes. The time limits we place on students' work are often fairly arbitrary.

It's not that students don't need time limits, but that our time limits don't have to be so rigid and exacting. When we can, we should give students some choice about how they spend their time. For instance, rather than always structuring classwork into a series of discrete tasks with rigidly enforced deadlines, try giving students a list of tasks to complete and letting them decide what they will work on first and how much time they will devote to each task, as long as they complete the work by the end of the period. Try designing homework assignments that span several nights so that students can choose when they will work on them.

Second, for most students, every second of their school day is scripted. More and more, we are encroaching on the few minutes of free time traditionally afforded: limiting recess so that students will spend more time "learning"; enforcing silent lunches under the auspices of "maintaining discipline"; mandating extra help during lunch, after school, and during specials such as music and PE to prepare for state tests; and removing electives so that students can spend more time on core subjects. However, the elimination of all free time during the school day makes it more likely that students will take little breaks throughout the class day—daydreaming during lessons, slacking off during group work, rushing through classwork so they can turn an assignment in early and get a few moments to themselves, or even skipping class altogether.

Although time on task is important, students do need small breaks to regroup, recharge, and refocus. You can build these breaks into the school day or into the rhythm of your class. Give students a few minutes to get up and stretch between activities, offer students some nights without homework (especially right before holiday breaks), or set aside one class period a month during which students are free to explore your subject in an unstructured way of their choosing.

Another way to give students more autonomy over their time is to show them how to manage their time better. What may look to us like procrastination is sometimes just students' underestimating how much time it will take them to complete tasks. Give students a sense of approximately how long it will take them to write a paper, finish a set of math problems, read a book chapter, or research a topic for social studies, and then help them manage their time so that they can complete the assignment by the deadline. Doing so will free up more discretionary time for students, and it will also give students a sense of control over their own time and ability to get things done. That sense of control and achievement can be very motivating. As they build this soft skill and become confident in using it, you can gradually remove your scaffolds.

Build In Team-Related Autonomy

With the rise of social networking, students' peer and friendship groups have become much less defined by geography, age, or even culture. In the digital world, they have an inexhaustible supply of teammates from which to choose. Contrast that with what happens in the classroom, where students generally work in predefined groups usually assigned by the teacher and very rarely get to pick their own teams.

I know, I know—students sometimes make bad choices about their teams, choosing their friends rather than teammates with complementary skills. But choice in this dimension of learning can be very motivating, and we have the opportunity to help students learn to make better choices.

Build In Technique-Related Autonomy

Imagine that you walk into work one day and your principal announces a new policy:

> *All teachers will now be held accountable for how well your students do on the upcoming standardized test. If any of your students fall below mastery, you will be fired. Additionally, all teachers will be required to teach using my new strategy. Look for the instructions in your mailbox. I will be around later today to observe each classroom and make sure that you are teaching according to my new strategy. Good luck.*

How do you think you'd feel about this new policy? (And to those of you who don't have to imagine your reaction because you work in a school with such a policy, I am really, really, sorry.) Would being held this accountable for results while being required to use a technique chosen for you motivate you to work harder? Is having this little control motivating, or does it just suck the motivation right out of you? Now think about how this scenario parallels the way in which we often hold students responsible for learning but rarely give them choice over how they learn.

When students have more autonomy over how they learn, they gravitate toward approaches that complement their own learning styles and learning preferences and that incorporate their currencies. In practical terms, providing more technique autonomy means giving students a choice of materials (textbook, an article, or a self-paced online tutorial?) and a choice of learning modality (work in small groups or alone? using manipulatives or a computer program?). The learning station approach, where students can learn about a topic a way that engages their currencies, is a good way to go about this.

While autonomy is very motivating, you do have to be careful. More autonomy does not mean an absence of structure, which can leave students paralyzed by the number of choices and the seeming lack of direction. Thus, give students autonomy within clearly defined structures and very clear parameters so that they are not overwhelmed by their freedom.

LEARN MORE Online

To learn how to set up leveled learning contracts that give students autonomy over task, time, team, and technique, visit www.mindstepsinc.com/motivation.

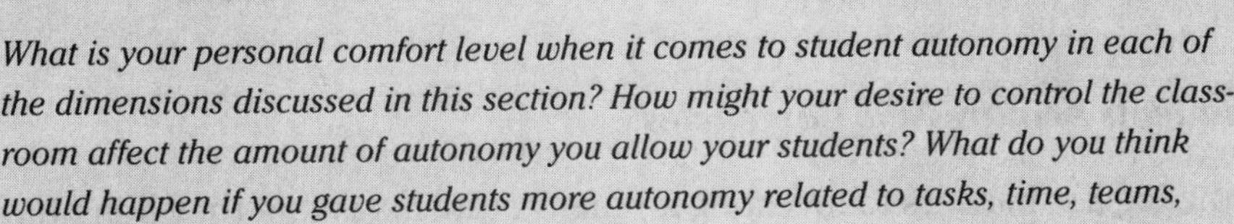

THINK ABOUT . . .

What is your personal comfort level when it comes to student autonomy in each of the dimensions discussed in this section? How might your desire to control the classroom affect the amount of autonomy you allow your students? What do you think would happen if you gave students more autonomy related to tasks, time, teams, and technique?

YOUR TURN

Acquire: How much autonomy do your students currently have over task, team, time, and technique? Identify one opportunity in each category to provide students with more autonomy in the classroom.

Apply: Think about a lesson you plan to teach in the next two weeks. Find one way to provide students with more autonomy in that lesson through choice related to the task, technique, team, or time.

Assimilate: In what ways are you currently giving students autonomy? Identify three or four specific ways you can up the degree of choice students have about task, team, time, and technique, and incorporate these new strategies into your current practice.

Adapt: Look for ways to combine the kinds of choices students have in your classroom. For instance, try reworking a current assignment to give students autonomy over both team and technique or over both timing and task.

Make Your Classroom Mastery Focused

One of the most powerful motivators is the sense of competence that comes with mastery. If the work in your classroom consists mainly of simple and not particularly interesting tasks, then it makes sense that a complicated series of rewards and punishments—carrots and sticks—*would* be helpful in getting students to do that work. But if you provide students with dynamic, interesting work that helps them use and build on currencies they have *and* acquire new and useful currencies, they will take up the tasks on their own, without the need for convincing or coercion. As students see that their investment has paid off in increased mastery, they become eager to invest more. Here are some strategies for making your classroom more mastery focused.

Help Students Acquire New Currencies

One of the biggest barriers to investing for many students is that they don't have the skills, knowledge, or behavioral know-how they need to engage in our classrooms. We cannot expect our students to arrive in our classes with all the currencies we value or that they will need. At some point, meeting the challenges we set will require them to acquire and master new skills, knowledge, and behaviors. Unfortunately, we often expect them to acquire these new currencies on their own.

It's far more practical and less frustrating to explicitly help students acquire new currencies. If students need to know how to study and take notes from a textbook in order to be successful in your class, take time to show them how to take notes. When your homework assignments are designed to provide important practice, but the students have difficulty remembering to complete their assignments, set up an organizational system that helps them remember, and establish homework buddies so that students can work together and hold each other accountable. If your students don't have the appropriate skills to pay attention during class, model the appropriate behavior, give them practice interacting appropriately, and set up classroom reminders to help them stay focused on their work. Helping your students acquire and use new currencies increases their ability to operate successfully in your classroom environment and school in general, promoting a sense of empowering mastery.

Teach Within the "Zone"

Challenge and rigor are essential to quality learning, but tasks requiring currencies students definitely do not possess are unlikely to increase motivation, especially if *they* are convinced that the task is outside their ability. At the same time, learning tasks that are too easy are also demotivating and quickly lead to boredom. Teaching within students' zone, where the work is neither too hard nor too easy, is one of the best ways to keep them engaged, appropriately challenged, and interested in what they are learning. In this zone, students can use their currencies and see the payoff of their investment.

Acknowledge Failure as Part of the Process

When you ask students to make an investment, especially students who don't have a history of successful investment, they will experience some failure along the way. Notice that I didn't say they "might" fail. Failure is inevitable. It is natural and necessary to learning. But surprisingly, we are often so intent on "selling" students on the benefits of the investment that we forget to tell them what we take for granted—that everything is hard before it is easy, and that the investment we are asking them to make will be hard at first and that it won't necessarily feel good. Pretending that learning is a linear and sanitized process doesn't prepare students for the inevitable failures they will face. Without the expectation of failure, students who hit a tough spot will be tempted to give up rather than know that what's required is a new plan that will ultimately lead to success. By creating the expectation of failure, you are helping students become more resilient.

Provide Growth-Oriented Feedback

Sadly, the message many students get in school is that they are either smart or not, and that the currencies they bring with them to school are all they'll ever have. Without realizing it, the kind of feedback we give can reinforce this fixed notion of intelligence. Calling students "*C* students" or "Honors kids," writing evaluative comments on students' papers ("You're a Rock Star!"), telling students they should "try harder" without telling them exactly how, or even classroom policies such as "no retakes" or inflexible ability grouping all convey a similar message to students: their ability to do well in school is fixed. Without meaning to, we blunt students' desire to try, take risks, and invest in their learning.

Growth-oriented feedback helps students understand that they can get smarter. Helping them see how to correct their mistakes, giving them opportunities for retakes with corrective action, writing coaching comments on their papers ("Great use of support here!"), and making specific comments that point out how their efforts directly affect their performance support the sense that if they make the right investment in the classroom, they *can* achieve mastery. If we can make our classrooms places where students know that they can get smarter and expand their knowledge and skills, they're more likely to invest their time, attention, and effort in our classrooms because they have experienced the payoffs of such investments.

THINK ABOUT . . .

In what ways do you currently promote competence in your classroom? What barriers might be blocking students' pathway to mastery? How can you remove these barriers?

YOUR TURN

Acquire: Think about the target investment you focused on in Chapter 1's Investment Analysis Worksheet. Identify the steps students will have to take in order to invest successfully. What specific actions or behaviors will they need to take or adopt to make this investment?

Apply: Think about the target investment you examined in Chapter 1's Investment Analysis Worksheet. What kind of feedback and support from you would help students make that investment? Identify the classroom adjustments you will have to make in order to make mastery more likely.

Assimilate: Think about the target investment you focused on in Chapter 1's Investment Analysis Worksheet. What is your students' current status relevant to making that investment? What can you do to help students master the skills, knowledge, or behaviors that will support successful investment?

Adapt: Think about the target investment you identified in Chapter 1's Investment Analysis Worksheet. What new currencies will your students need in order to invest successfully? Identify how you will help students acquire those new currencies in the course of your daily classroom interactions.

Promote a Sense of Purpose

For a long time, conventional wisdom held that grades were the best way to motivate students. Going to school was all about getting good grades, passing tests, and making the honor roll. For 21st-century learners, grades are no longer enough. Students are redefining what success in school means for them, and many are determining that grades are not a sufficient reward for their investment. What they want is a sense of purpose. They want to know how what they are learning in school is going to be useful to their lives outside school. The following are several ways you can build a classroom that offers students that sense of purpose.

Focus on the "What" and *the "Why"*

In the past, it was sufficient to tell students only what they were going to learn; the "why" was assumed ("because I said so"). Today's students, however, want to understand why they are studying what they're studying and how their investment will help them learn it. It's up to us to make that case explicitly, going beyond writing mastery objectives on the board to state plainly, "We are learning this because ______." Start every class session by helping students understand what they will learn, why they will be learning it, and how learning it will help them achieve something valuable to them.

Remember, what your students value may be very different from what you value, and this means you may have to dig a little to arrive at the right "why." For instance, it may be true that learning algebra will help students in college, but for students who are not interested in going to college or for whom college is still a fuzzy goal, it may not be very motivating. Explaining that learning algebra helps a person solve all kinds of problems, even ones that have nothing to do with math, might be a more effective approach.

Connect Specific School Tasks to Higher Goals

Researchers point out that the greater the congruence between task-specific, behaviorally based goals ("I want to complete my homework") and higher, more abstract goals ("I want to learn about fractions"), the more likely it is that a student will be engaged. Our classroom environments can make that connection much more obvious for students.

As you give each assignment, tell students why the work will help them reach the day's objective and the larger learning goal beyond that. Connect assignments or activities so that students can move progressively toward learning goals—some that you set, based on standards, and some that they set themselves. Then get students involved in tracking and reflecting on the progress they make. Doing all of this will reinforce students' sense of purpose, redirecting focus away from external rewards, such as grades and test scores, and toward what really matters to them. When they have a meaningful purpose for their investment, they are more likely to make it.

Help Students Expand Their Identities

Consider how many times you've said to yourself, "If only my students understood how *not* doing their homework is hurting them, they would do it" or "If they understood how important good grades are in getting scholarships, they would work harder to make good grades." How many times have you taken pains to explain to students what they stand to gain (or lose) from investing themselves in the classroom, but still their behavior does not change?

When people make choices, they tend to use one of two basic models of decision making. The first is what's called the "consequences model," and it involves a person weighing the costs and benefits of the options and choosing whatever option seems most likely to have a positive, needs-meeting outcome. The second is called the "identity model," and it involves a person making a decision based on "what someone like me would do" (March, 1994). Most motivation efforts in schools assume students make investment decisions by using the consequence model, weighing the pros and cons of their investment. However, many unmotivated students are making investment decisions using an identity model. That means that instead of trying to get students to understand why they should or should not do something, we should try motivating them by appealing to their identity.

First, start by helping students project themselves into examples. Leading phrases, such as "Suppose you were trying to figure out how to keep the southern states from seceding from the union . . ." and "What would you do if you were the character in this story?" can help students see themselves as a part of the example and think through how they might use their currencies to invest in that experience.

Second, try helping them cultivate new "student identities"—new ways of thinking of themselves as learners. Some of this involves changing the kind of work you give them, but it rests to a remarkable degree on the kinds of words you use to describe students and to describe what goes on in your classroom. I have seen teachers take groups of failing 9th graders and put them on the track to advanced classes by shifting to an "honors"-level curriculum and giving students more challenging work. I have seen teachers take a group of failing 3rd graders and turn them into *A* students by forming "elite" after-school "Scholars Sessions," where students learn brain-friendly study skills. I have seen teachers turn disruptive students into "classroom monitors," cliques into "study groups," late work into "missed opportunities," wrong answers into "nonexamples," and fixed abilities into "currencies" students can trade, acquire, and spend.

When you use renaming to adjust your classroom environment, you help to change students' perceptions of who they are and what they can do. For example, a "disruptive student" is not very likely to make a positive contribution to the class, but a "classroom monitor" seems like someone who can be counted on. A "clique" is focused on gossip, but a "study group" is focused on studying. "Late work" means a missed deadline, but "missed opportunities" suggests something more valuable. For many students, a "wrong answer" means "I am not smart," but a "nonexample" means "I have the chance to get it right." Finally, "abilities" are things that are fixed, but "currencies" can be acquired and used through planning and choice.

New identities can give students a new sense of purpose and a new attitude toward investment. They begin to think, "I am not doing this because I want to gain a reward or avoid punishment; I am doing this because *this is what people like me do.*"

THINK ABOUT . . .

What do you currently do to give students a sense of purpose in your classroom? What changes could you make to your classroom structures to give students a greater sense of purpose? How will doing so make students more likely to invest?

YOUR TURN

Acquire: Think about the target investment you identified in Chapter 1 and focus on why you are asking students to make it. Identify which of these reasons are most likely to offer students a sense of purpose.

Apply: Take the strategies for building a sense of purpose and apply them to the target investment you identified in Chapter 1. Identify specific ways you might help students understand why the investment is important, connect the investment to some of their higher goals, and use the investment opportunity to help them cultivate new student identities.

Assimilate: What do you currently do to build a sense of purpose into your classroom activities? Examine your current practices and identify at least one strategy you might use to increase students' sense of purpose, particularly with regard to the target investment you identified in Chapter 1.

Adapt: Examine your reasons for asking students to make the target investment you identified in Chapter 1. Identify specific ways your reasons for wanting the investment may differ from your students' reasons for making the investment. How might the differences affect the way that you communicate purpose to these students?

Promote a Sense of Belonging

When students feel that they are accepted and respected by their teacher and peers—when they feel like they belong in your classroom—they tend to be more interested in the material and activities, and to have a greater sense that they can and will be successful in school. If we want students to invest in our class, we have to help them feel that they belong to our classroom community.

Forge Authentic Relationships with Students

There is a lot of really bad advice out there about how to "connect" with students—everything from pretending to like them to inserting pop culture references in your lessons. Such advice is really geared toward manipulating students by making them think that you know them. Instead, take time to really get to know your students: who they are, what they want, what they are afraid of, and what currencies they bring with them to the classroom. The more you pay attention to your students, the more opportunities you will find to understand them and connect with them in meaningful way.

Authentic relationships are never one-sided. You cannot truly get to know and care about your students if they also don't get a chance to know you and care about you. I don't mean that you must come in on every Monday and dish about your weekend or show them your body piercings. I simply mean that you must be yourself. A lot of times we try to be our idea of what a teacher should be instead of just being ourselves. It's a fine line to walk here. You must still be the adult, but you can also be human. Acknowledge your mistakes, laugh sometimes, smile at your students, let them see you being passionate about something. Showing a full picture of who you are helps them relax, shed some of their armor, and learn to trust you.

Use Cooperative Learning

So many classrooms focus on individual achievement even though, outside the classroom, both the real world and the virtual world are becoming increasingly collaborative. When they're not in school, students gather in formal and informal affinity groups—sometimes in person and increasingly online—to play games, examine shared interests, and explore hobbies. They are members of multiple social networks and use these networks to do everything from forge friendships to get recommendations on new music or movies to find new resources and learning. If we want to motivate 21st-century learners, we must move away from individualistic classrooms to classrooms that foster the connectedness and belonging our students seek.

Cooperative learning is an intriguing option. It allows students to work together, leveraging their various currencies to solve problems. I am not talking here of the kind of "group work" that involves students pushing their desks into clusters of threes and fours and completing individual worksheets; I am talking about opportunities for students to collaborate for the purpose of exploring and solving intriguing problems. To be effective, cooperative learning activities must have a defined goal, allow students to use their individual currencies to help the group reach that goal, and allow students to learn from one other. The more they see that their currencies are valued both by you and by their classmates, the more likely they are to invest those currencies in the classroom.

Teach Students to Code-Switch

Too often, the investments we ask students to make in the classroom require them to set aside the currencies they use within their families and communities and take up our currencies instead. Students might be asked to abandon the way that they talk at home for the "proper English" of school or to raise a hand before speaking, when the way to be heard at home is to talk the loudest and refuse to cede the floor. Many students resist investing in school because doing so requires them to shed the very currencies that signal their belonging to their home cultures.

The way to help students choose to belong to our classrooms is not to ask them to lose their home cultures and the behaviors and ways of communicating that go along with them, but to show them how to *code-switch.* Code-switching is simply a way to move among several different groups. In the same way that I use dollars and English when I am in the United States, euros and French when I am in France, and pesos and Spanish when I am in Mexico, I use different registers of English and different behaviors depending on whether I am in school, at work, at home, or out with my friends. Code-switching allows me to belong to several cultures without giving up any one culture for another.

Thus, rather than tell students that their way of doing things is wrong, help them understand that different contexts demand different sets of currencies. What's appropriate and useful in one dimension of their lives may be inappropriate for the classroom, another dimension of their lives. For instance, if students speak a particular vernacular or slang, don't tell them that their way of speaking is "wrong"; point out that it's simply "not the language we use in the classroom," and ask them to translate what they're saying into language that *is* appropriate for the classroom. If students use behavior that is inappropriate for the classroom, don't judge the behavior; simply ask them translate their behavior to behavior that is more appropriate for the classroom. Talking directly about code-switching and making it part of your curriculum not only helps students navigate school cultures much more easily, it shows them how to be insiders rather than outsiders and helps them find a place to belong within your classroom.

THINK ABOUT . . .

What are some ways you currently work to foster students' sense of belonging in the classroom? What else might you do?

YOUR TURN

Acquire: Think about your target investment. What specific things might you do to create a sense of belonging that would induce students to make that investment?

Apply: Look for specific ways that you can leverage a sense of belonging to help students make your target investment. Then, adjust your classroom practices accordingly to support these investment efforts.

Assimilate: Identify the ways that you already work to create a sense of belonging for every student in your classroom. How might those structures support your target investment? What other structures could you put in place or what tweaks to your current structure could you make to further foster a sense of belonging for all of your students?

Adapt: Think specifically about your reluctant and resistant students. In which ways do they not seem to be connecting to other students in the classroom? Adapt the strategies you currently use to create a sense of belonging to help these students develop a deeper sense of belonging in your classroom.

CHECKPOINT SUMMARY

Classrooms Worth Investing In Offer Students	Strategies to Try
Autonomy	• Give students choices over time, task, team, and technique.
Opportunities for mastery	• Help students acquire new currencies. • Teach within the zone. • Make failure a part of the process. • Provide growth-oriented feedback.
A sense of purpose	• Focus on the "what" *and* the "why." • Connect tasks to students' goals. • Help students expand their identities.
A sense of belonging	• Create academically oriented affinity groups. • Show students how to code-switch.

Focusing on Your Classroom

Now it's time to take the investment you identified in Chapter 1 and examine it through the lens of your own classroom. What classroom structures do you already have in place to make the investment more likely? What other structures could you implement to support motivation? Use the **Classroom Climate Worksheet** on page 63 to help you identify how you can create a classroom environment that will best support investment.

YES, BUT . . .

How will I get students to attempt an investment when they are so reluctant already?

It's true that even when you remove barriers to investment, students may still be hesitant to engage, especially if they lack some of the classroom currencies and have a history of failure. It's also true that most learning involves some lag time between the effort invested up front and the progress and benefits that this effort will bring. If the lag time is too great, the student will simply check out.

Classroom Climate Worksheet

Target Investment:	
Classroom Barriers Which classroom barriers make it difficult for students to make the target investment you are asking for?	
Autonomy What can you do to give students a greater sense of autonomy? How will a sense of autonomy help students invest more successfully?	
Mastery What can you do to give students a greater sense of mastery as they are making the target investment?	
Purpose How will the target investment foster a sense of purpose? How will that sense of purpose make further investment more likely?	
Belonging What classroom structures can you put into place to help students feel a sense of connection and belonging? How might this sense of belonging help students invest in your classroom?	
Plan for Structural Change Based on your answers above, what specific changes can you make in your classroom to help reluctant learners make the target investment?	

 This worksheet is available for download at www.mindstepsinc.com/motivation.

Cognitive scientists talk about *amplification of output,* which is when a student invests a small input and gets a much larger output in return. This happens all the time in the classrooms of master teachers. At a certain point, things "click": students suddenly grasp a concept and all kinds of learning falls into place, or they understand a nuance and can now solve all sorts of math problems much more quickly and easily.

I recommend a two-step approach to carry students over the time delay between investment and return. First, talk directly to your students about the connection between effort and payoff. Stress that making small adjustments or grasping a key idea can make their effort more effective; they may be a lot closer to understanding than they think. Second, provide positive reinforcement for the effort they do invest—even the small effort. Remember that the payoff of investment that students are seeing doesn't have to be a big reward or even that "aha!" moment of learning. It can also be the satisfaction of doing something well or the jolt that comes from overcoming an obstacle. Provide payoff through specific praise. Instead of a generic "Great job!" give students praise that makes the connection between their effort and the payoff very clear. Here are some examples:

- "Wow! Look at how by just setting aside 15 minutes to study these flashcards, you raised your vocabulary quiz score by 20 points!"
- "See how by using this graphic organizer, your notes are so much better organized? I bet tonight you will have a much easier time remembering what we discussed today when you study."
- "Look at that! By just taking five minutes to focus on your work instead of talking, you are almost finished!"
- "See how scanning the headings first made reading this chapter so much easier? I bet you feel smarter already!"
- "You spent 10 minutes going over your notes last night. Look how much smarter you got!"

Specific praise helps students recognize the intangible payoffs for their efforts and reinforces their intrinsic motivation to make future investments.

3

Understanding and Addressing Student Resistance

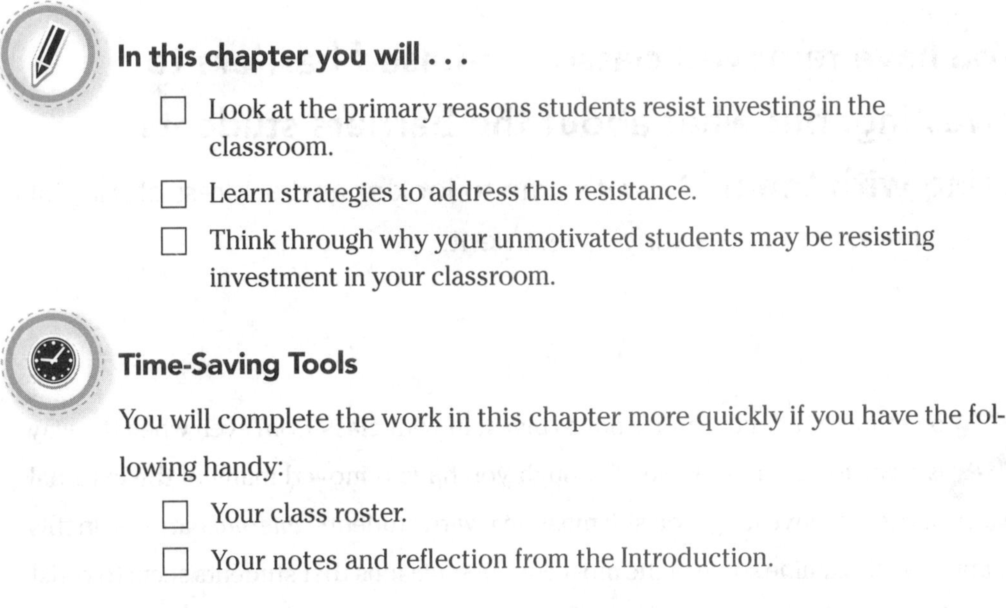

In this chapter you will . . .

- ☐ Look at the primary reasons students resist investing in the classroom.
- ☐ Learn strategies to address this resistance.
- ☐ Think through why your unmotivated students may be resisting investment in your classroom.

Time-Saving Tools

You will complete the work in this chapter more quickly if you have the following handy:

- ☐ Your class roster.
- ☐ Your notes and reflection from the Introduction.

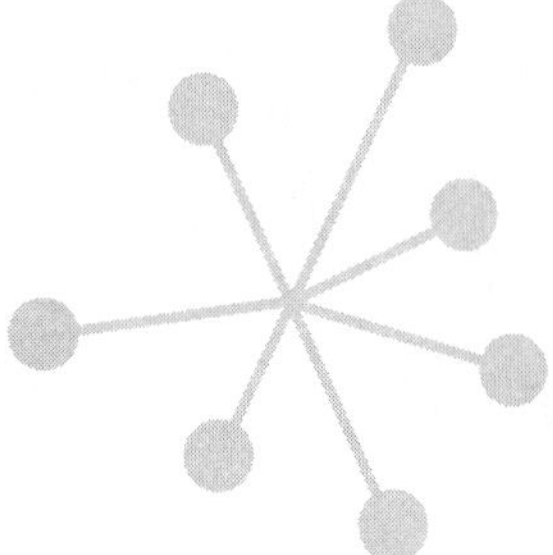

You have removed classroom-based barriers to investing, but what about the barriers students bring with them? Now it's time to look at and address students' internal reasons for resisting investment.

Sometimes students choose not to invest in your classroom even when the way is clear for them to do so. Although you have removed many of the external barriers to investing, you still must deal with students' *internal* barriers. In this chapter, we'll examine some of the most common reasons that students seem to resist our efforts to help them learn and the strategies you can use to try to break through these internal barriers.

Why Students Resist Investing

Suppose you have a car for sale, and you're hoping I will buy it. As the prospective buyer, I must ask myself several questions. Do I really want a car? Do I want *your* car? Can I afford your car? Will I enjoy driving your car? Do I trust you to give me a fair deal? All these questions run through my head before I decide to lay down my money.

The same kind of dilemma exists in the classroom every day. We offer a curriculum and opportunities to learn it. Our students consider our offer and then decide whether it is worth their investment. Anytime a student chooses to engage in the classroom, that student has made a value judgment and decided that engaging will provide something of value, either now or down the line. If students cannot see the value in what we are asking them to do, they will not invest. Likewise, if students don't value what we offer them—not just our curriculum, but also our teaching style, strategies, classroom rules, and daily procedures—they will resist our efforts to help them learn. And if students don't value the currencies that school in general offers them, they will disengage from school altogether.

When we don't start where our students are or spend enough time seeking the root causes of our students' resistance, we tend to jump ahead to trying to fix the problem, which often means working to convince students that they need to do their work or looking for ways to make the work more attractive to students. More often than not, this tends to be a frustrating path, involving lots of effort on our part for too little gain. If you do not understand why your students resist engaging in your classroom, you will never build consistent motivation.

There are three primary reasons students resist learning, and all three have to do with value:

- *Fear of failure:* They don't see the value in putting forth the effort investment requires.
- *Lack of relevance:* They don't see the value in the content itself.
- *Lack of trust:* They don't see the value in you, their teacher.

Root Cause #1: Fear of Failure

Classroom investment is always something of a gamble for students. There's no guarantee, for example, that hard work will translate into academic success, that paying attention during a lesson will lead to instant understanding, or that a careful reading of the assigned novel will lead to personal illumination or even enjoyment. And the negative feelings and repercussions some students associate with failure can make investment seem like an even worse bet.

Students who disengage because of a fear of failure are not a uniform lot. Some have a history of failure, and the idea of *further* failure can be so upsetting that they sometimes won't even attempt an assignment, even if they already have the currencies they need to be successful. It's the same way that many of us might have a decent poker hand but be inclined to fold as the stakes get higher. Other students fear failure because they cannot see how they can acquire the currencies they need to invest successfully. If what we ask seems out of reach—and failure feels inevitable—there are lots of students who would rather not try at all. Even students who do not have a history of failure may develop a fear of failure, especially if they have breezed through earlier grades and suddenly face more rigorous coursework that requires increased effort. They may begin to shut down, afraid that if they try, everyone will find out that they are not as smart as they seemed.

Disengagement resulting from a fear of failure is due to what Dweck (2006) calls a "fixed mindset." She argues that students have one of two predominant mindsets when it comes to intelligence. Either they believe that intelligence is fixed, meaning that there is nothing they can do to get smarter, or they believe that intelligence is elastic, meaning that they can grow more intelligent through effective effort. Students who refuse to try for fear of failing tend to believe that they are either smart or not smart, and they can be reluctant to take on new challenges that may reveal them to be the latter.

The thing we forget about this kind of disengagement is that it is a relatively healthy coping behavior. Rather than stay in a state of frustration and hopelessness and expend needless energy pursuing an unattainable goal, students who disengage conserve their energy and use it to pursue different, more attainable goals. This kind of disengagement is also self-protective behavior. It is much easier to say, "I failed because I didn't try," than to say, "I tried my best and still failed."

Identifying Resistance Related to Fear of Failure

When trying to determine which of your disengaged students may be resisting investment due to a fear of failure, look for the following characteristics:

- They refuse to try, even with supports.
- They give up easily.
- They turn in incomplete work.
- They tend to procrastinate.
- They regularly seek reassurance.
- The more you push them, the harder they resist.
- They seem to expect to fail.
- They are either very grade-conscious or pretend that they don't care about grades at all.
- They avoid situations where they might look "stupid."
- They blame failure on things they cannot control.

- They are likely to cheat under pressure.
- They focus on how "easy" or "hard" a task is.

Root Cause #2: Lack of Relevance

For many 21st-century learners, all of school—from the way the day is structured to the type of work they are doing to the policies and procedures in the classroom—seems archaic. The disconnect between "school stuff" and "real life" can be even more dramatic for traditionally underrepresented students in schools that are dominated by the majority culture and are vastly different from their home experiences. When students cannot see the value in the content in terms of their own lives, this *lack of relevance* leads to disengagement.

Generally speaking, teachers intuitively understand the disconnect that exists between school life and our students' real lives, and most of us do try to demonstrate the relevance of what we ask students to do. We attempt to "connect" with our students by playing getting-to-know-you games to understand their likes and dislikes, their interests and hobbies. We read articles about 21st-century learning styles, or we attend cultural competence seminars in an attempt to understand students who are different from us. We try to find connections between our curriculum and their lives. However, such efforts can quickly become superficial. Can you really effectively get to know all 20 to 35 students in your classroom or make a personal connection with each one fast enough or deeply enough to help each student find a way to access the curriculum? Can a seminar or an article really give you an in-depth understanding of your students' experiences and culture? And even if you do come to understand your students better through these means, can you really make logical connections between the curriculum and their lives every single lesson, every single day? Our students may be amused by our attempts to discuss with them the latest hip-hop hit or the plot of their favorite television shows, but will these discussions help us get them to connect with a curriculum that is not always immediately relevant to their world, especially when we don't understand their worlds particularly well?

For some students, a lack of relevance will lead to boredom. Sitting in class and learning in ways that are often linear and passive can seem like a long, slow trudge when they are used to spending their out-of-school hours engaging in multiple tasks at once or in activities like sports and gaming, which provide constant stimulation, escalating challenge, and immediate gratification. If they cannot see the relevance of what they are learning or how they are being asked to learn, it simply will not interest them, and they will invest.

Another, more sneaky form of disengagement due to a lack of relevance arises when students, especially those who are used to instant gratification, choose not to invest in the classroom because doing so requires delaying gratification. Telling a 3rd grader that he should work hard at an assignment because what he's learning will pay off in high school and college is not only developmentally inappropriate, it's just plain foolish. Imagine if I told you not to eat that doughnut in your hand because eating it will significantly affect your health when you are 80. How much weight would that carry in your decision to indulge? If students cannot expect a specific and immediate return on their investment, many won't see the value in putting forth the effort.

Identifying Resistance Related to Lack of Relevance

When trying to figure out which of your disengaged students may be resisting investment due to a lack of relevance, look for these behaviors:

- They turn in incomplete or shoddy work.
- They complain that the assignment is too easy or boring.
- They ask, "Will this be on the test?"
- They doodle, daydream, or engage in distracting behaviors.
- They look for shortcuts.
- They seem not to care about their own learning.
- They fail to see the connection between their work and their ultimate success.
- They focus on the grade rather than the learning.
- They rush through assignments, investing little time or thought in the work.

Root Cause #3: Lack of Trust

Sometimes students are waiting to see whether you will invest in them before they choose to invest in you. This is especially true if students feel that you don't value the currencies they bring to the classroom. I know it's frustrating to continually work hard to help students, only to have them resist your best efforts. Many teachers simply give up, but that is exactly what many resistant learners are hoping you will do. They know that if they wait you out and exhaust your efforts, you will leave them alone.

Often, these students are withholding their currencies because they don't trust you to help them use their currencies to meet their needs. It's not that they don't want to invest in the class; they don't want to invest in *you*. They don't value you, don't believe that you can or will help them be successful, and don't think that you care enough about them as individuals to make their investment worthwhile.

Identifying Resistance Related to Lack of Trust

When trying to figure out which of your disengaged students may be resisting investment because they don't trust you to help them be successful, look for these behaviors:

- They are oppositional, defiant, or angry.
- They do things to intentionally annoy you.
- They take your comments about their performance personally.
- They blame you for their poor grades.
- They refuse to follow class rules and procedures.
- They do not access the supports you have in place already.

Addressing Students' Resistance

Given that students make investment decisions based on value, if we want to overcome their resistance, we must demonstrate value in a way they can understand. One of the biggest mistakes we can make is to try to motivate students using generic strategies. Instead, tailor your response to directly address the root cause of students' resistance and build value in students' own terms.

Address Fear of Failure by Building Resilience

Resilience is the ability to bounce back from failure. In order for students to attempt difficult work or take risks in the classroom, they have to feel that there is *some hope* of their being successful. If your students are not investing because they are afraid to fail, there are several things you can do to help them overcome their fears.

Link Currencies Students Have to Currencies the Investment Requires

One of the most motivating things we can do for students is to show them how to turn their seeming disadvantages into advantages. Be explicit about how what they are learning connects to what they know already. Show them how to take what they already know and use it to learn and be successful on *this* project or *this* assignment.

Treat Failure as an Opportunity

Students need to understand that failure is inevitable—a natural, necessary, and temporary part of all learning. Stress this idea continually in your classroom, and be sure to keep it in mind when you provide feedback on student performance.

Plan Ahead to Develop Currencies Before They Are Needed

Building students confidence and sense of competence will make them more willing to take risks. So, for example, preteach vocabulary before students will need to understand and use those words for an assignment, and treat social-skill and soft-skill currencies that will support effective learning as you would any other vital part of the curriculum. As students build their repertoire of currencies and shift to a growth mindset, they will be less afraid of investing in the classroom. (For more on helping students develop necessary skills, see the *How to Support Struggling Students* guide in this series.)

Build In More Opportunities to Practice

Practice helps boost students' confidence and prepare them to take on a test, classroom presentation, or major assignment. Showing students how to practice effectively helps students develop a growth mindset. They learn that they can grow smarter with the right kind of practice.

Provide Detailed Feedback

Detailed feedback gives students the information they need to learn from mistakes. Be explicit about how students can use other currencies to make their efforts more efficient, and clarify how doing so will increase their success.

Lower the Cost of Failure

Allow retakes, assignment resubmissions, and opportunities for students to have some say over the difficulty level of their assignment. You might do this on a temporary basis, implementing what Erik Erikson describes as a "psychosocial moratorium," or you might build such measures into your classroom policy. Another way to lower the cost of failure is to shift to a grading system that limits grades to *A*, *B*, and *Not Yet* designations to underscore that if students don't get it right the first time, they will have another chance.

Address Lack of Relevance Through Personalization

If the root cause of your students' resistance to investing is that they do not see value in the content, the best way to address their resistance is by clarifying *personal relevance*. Students need to understand why doing the tasks and behaviors you're asking for are important—not important in a general way, but important to *them*. Despite how they may behave, they all have goals of some kind; they all want to be something more than who they are now. It's a matter of finding out what students value and linking the investment you might be asking for (improved reading, so that they will pass the state test) to a payoff that they desire (being able to keep up with the increasing length and complexity of the books in the Harry Potter series). To illustrate further, students may not care about learning effective study habits in order to pass your science test, but they might be willing to invest in the learning if they can grasp that having more effective study habits means they'll need to spend less time studying.

Remember, investing is purposeful. One student may study because she believes that doing so will help her earn the *A* she wants. Another may pay attention because he believes doing so will earn him your approval. A third may read the assigned book because he is interested in the topic and enjoys reading about it. The students who choose not to make these investments do so because they do not believe these investments will help them achieve any of their purposes or goals. When students ask questions like "Is this going to be on the test?" they are asking a value question. They are really asking, "What's the payoff on my investment for writing this down and remembering it?" When students ask questions like "How will this help me in life?" they are again asking a value question. They want to know how a topic or skill is meaningful to them either now or in the future.

Until we help students see how their investment can meet their needs, we haven't demonstrated relevance. The key to addressing this resistance is to demonstrate value in *their terms,* not yours. Think about value from the students' perspective—not only what's in it for them, but what *they* will think is in it for them. Rather than talk about how working hard now will help the student do well in college (which may be a sign of your currencies and not the students'), talk about how working hard will help the student feel a sense of accomplishment for overcoming a really difficult task. Rather than focus on the intrinsic benefits of a job well done, show students how doing things right the first time saves them trouble later on. When demonstrating value, make sure that you don't allow your own values to overshadow your ability to see the value through your students' eyes.

Allow Students to Learn in Ways That Are Most Effective for Them

Design assignments that allow your students to apply their skills, strengths, culture, and background knowledge to successfully invest in learning. The goal is to get these students to feel comfortable in the classroom and see it as a place where they belong.

Stress Long-Term Gains

Of course, many of the investments you'll ask students to make do not have an immediate payoff but do require what seem like immediate sacrifices. Maybe the students have to give up having fun and buckle down and study. Or they have to let go of certain friendships in order to stay out of trouble. But if we can show them how their investment will help them achieve a goal, we can often build value in the investment even when it feels like a sacrifice. This means, for example, showing students how investing in doing quality work the first time saves them time in the long run, or how not doing their work is actually making their lives less fun because they have to stay in at recess to make up work rather than play with their friends. By showing students how investing their currencies as you recommend will help them acquire or achieve something they want, you can help them choose to make the investment even if the tasks involved are not immediately gratifying.

Generate Curiosity

We often try to address the "But it's so boring!" problem by dressing up our subjects in order to make them seem as appealing, fun, or entertaining as we can. However, most studies on motivation have found very little evidence that students' interest in a subject or activity is a determinant of learning (Parker & Lepper, 1992). What this means is that although students may initially find an activity boring, it doesn't mean that they will *always* find it so. Students' interest can build over time if they feel that they are learning something from the activity, improving their skills, or coming closer to mastering it. In other words, motivation can grow over time. The challenge, of course, is to get students to pay attention or engage in the process long enough for that motivation to take root. Two strategies can help.

First, get the ball rolling by using story structure to present material. A story provides context and relevance that is often missing in most school subjects. Because a story puts what we are asking students to learn into a framework that is more like their day-to-day experiences, it helps them see in a very real way how what we want them to learn is relevant to their lives and to the currencies they value.

Story structure can be used in a variety of ways. Introduce a new unit by telling a story that illustrates a key concept or a critical dilemma that you will spend the unit trying to solve. During a social studies lesson, start by telling the story of a key player in a historical event as a way of illustrating the dilemma and helping students make a connection to history itself. Before reading a story or a novel, ask students to imagine a time when they faced a similar dilemma as the protagonist. At the beginning of a math lesson, give students a real-life example in story form in which a particular mathematical procedure helps them solve a problem or understand a phenomenon. In science, take good and bad bacteria and turn them into heroes and villains. Draw students in by creating stories.

A second strategy for generating curiosity is to choose activities and concepts that create disequilibria. Presenting discrepant ideas—ideas that conflict with students' prior knowledge or beliefs—often prompts students to seek information that will resolve the discrepancy. It is best to use moderate discrepancies, because they are easily incorporated into a student's mental framework; large discrepancies may be rapidly discounted. For instance, typically bored students may be roused to initial interest if you begin a science unit by telling them that they don't catch a cold from not wearing a hat in winter or from going outside with wet hair. Once you have their attention with these surprising facts, you can go on to explain to them the idea of viruses and how they work.

If you can spark students' initial interest through the use of story structure or discrepant ideas, and if you can then create learning tasks that build on this initial interest by helping students develop their currencies successfully, you can usually overcome initial boredom to build students' motivation over time.

Deliberately Build Students' Capacity for Delayed Gratification

In a society that offers instant gratification at every turn, delaying gratification is a skill that must be cultivated in students over time. The way to start is to connect anything that requires delayed gratification to an immediate reward. For instance, last year, I bought a treadmill. It sat in the box for a month, and then after I unpacked it, it sat unused for another month. I recognized the value in working out (after all, I'd paid for the treadmill). But recognizing the value was not enough. The payoff—better health—was too vague, and the weight loss I was aiming for was too far down the road to make me climb on the thing after a long trip or a busy day at work. It wasn't until I connected walking on the treadmill to something else I enjoy that I was able to be consistent. In my case, I record all the shows I miss when I am traveling and watch them when I return. I made a deal with myself that I can only watch those shows while I am on the treadmill. Now I can't wait to get on the treadmill to watch my shows. Should I get on the treadmill for the health benefits? Absolutely. But will I? Not likely. Connecting the treadmill to something else I valued and could enjoy immediately was key.

The same is true of our students, and here is where currencies can help. Rather than fight with your resistant learners to try to convince them to invest in something with a long-term payoff, try connecting the activity with a more immediate reward in a form of currency they value. For instance, if students value grades as a currency and won't work unless they earn a grade, take a long-term assignment and break it up into smaller parts, assigning a grade for each part. Or if students value working together, build cooperative opportunities into the long-term assignment. Perhaps your students value connecting with you? Schedule one-on-one or small-group conferences after each milestone of a long-term project to review what students have done so far and discuss what is still left to do.

We all make this kind of tradeoff all the time. We tell ourselves that if we just grade five more papers, we can relax and watch television. Or we find ways to reward ourselves along the way. We celebrate when we are halfway through our master's degree coursework or as we finish each chapter of our dissertation. We build our own capacity to delay gratification and keep ourselves motivated during a long and difficult task, especially when the ultimate payoff is in the distant future. If we need to find ways to help ourselves to stay motivated during a long task, certainly our students (who, given the instantaneous nature of the 21st century, are unused to delaying gratification) do, too.

Focus Students on the Immediate, Emotional Rewards of Investing

Another way to demonstrate that an investment is relevant to students' lives right now is to show them how much better they will feel if they make the investment. Often, we make a logical case for learning ("It will help you get good grades"; "You'll need to know this for middle and high school"; "You'll be able to get into a good college") but neglect to make the emotional case. This is why sometimes students may understand that they ought to invest and still not be motivated to make the investment.

Students need to understand why making the investment is so important—not in a general way or an abstract, someday-way, but important to *them* right now. Call their attention to how their investment will enhance their lives: "You will feel so much smarter"; "Learning this is fun"; "Being able to do this feels good."

Address Lack of Trust by Building Relationships

If you want your students to invest in your classroom, you must invest in them first. Only when students realize that you are not going to give up on them and that you genuinely care about their progress will they begin to invest in you. Their investments may seem small at first and not nearly equal to the investment that you have made in them, but over time, they will invest if you demonstrate that you can and want to help them be successful. There are several ways to do this.

Communicate Clear Goals with High Expectations

Vague and ambiguous goals create anxiety in students. Show students that you have a clear vision for where the class is headed, and explain to your students that you have a plan for how you will get them to that goal. Communicate that you are confident that you can help students reach the goals and standards of the course.

Create Support Structures That Help Students Invest Successfully

Scaffold students' new learning and provide proactive interventions that help them make consistent progress toward their goals. Communicate your intervention plan from the very beginning in order to show students that you have thought through their needs and are ready to provide assistance. In a sense, you're letting students know that there is a safety net in place. (For more on how to build proactive supports, see the *How to Support Struggling Students* guide in this series.)

Show Students How to Leverage Currencies They Have

For instance, many students spend a lot of their time texting. In fact, they have developed an entire system of shorthand in order to text more quickly. Why not show students how they can use that same shorthand to take more effective notes? Leverage reduces the amount of work involved, or at the very least, the students' *perception* of the amount of work required, by helping students find a match between what they know how to do already and the investment you are asking them to make. Thus, you don't just ask students to do a series of math problems for homework. You also show them a shortcut for solving the math problems that makes homework go much faster from here on out. Instead of asking students to study alone for an upcoming test, you group students into study groups where they can work together and learn from each other and share resources. In this way, you are building trust with your students by demonstrating to them that you are not just going to ask for an investment and leave them on their own to figure out how; you are going to show them how to make the investment successfully.

Give Forward-Focused, Growth-Oriented Feedback

Inspire your students further with feedback that doesn't just evaluate how well they are using their present currencies but also shows them how to get even better. When students see that your feedback is helpful, they will develop more trust in your ability to assist them in getting where they want to go.

CHECKPOINT SUMMARY

Students Resist Investing Because	Strategies to Try
They fear failure.	• Link currencies students have to the currencies the investment requires. • Treat failure as an opportunity. • Plan ahead to develop currencies before students need them. • Build in more opportunities to practice. • Provide detailed feedback designed to help students learn from mistakes. • Allow retakes, assignment resubmissions, and opportunities for students to have some say over the difficulty level of their assignment.
The investment seems irrelevant to their lives.	• Point out real relevance. • Allow students to learn in ways that are most effective for them. • Show students how the investment will matter to them. • Stress long-term gains. • Generate curiosity with story structures and by creating disequilibria. • Break long-term tasks into smaller ones with payoffs in currencies that students value. • Focus students on the immediate, emotional rewards of investing.
They don't feel you are invested in them.	• Invest in them first. • Communicate clear goals with high expectations. • Create support structures that help students invest successfully. • Show students how to leverage currencies they have. • Give forward-focused, growth-oriented feedback.

THINK ABOUT . . .

Take a look at your student roster and the notes you've made about your disengaged students. Which of the root causes of resistance do you associate with these students?

YOUR TURN

Acquire: Think about your most unmotivated students and the investment you want them to make in your classroom. Determine which of the three root causes discussed may be at the heart of their resistance.

Apply: Think about your most unmotivated students and the target investment you want them to make in your classroom. Identify the root cause or causes of their resistance, and try one or more of the strategies mentioned to address this barrier and demonstrate value in their terms.

Assimilate: Think about the target investment you want students to make in your classroom. Of the three root causes for students' resistance to investing, which one tends to be the biggest barrier to investing for your students? Reflect on the strategies you already use to address their resistance and how effective these strategies have been in the past. Select one ineffective strategy you've tried, discard it, and replace it with one additional strategy from the suggestions in this section.

Adapt: Think about the three root causes for resisting investing in the classroom. List the ways that these root causes manifest themselves with your students. What patterns do you notice? What types of assignments, classroom procedures, rules of engagement, and interactions tend to contribute to this resistance? Identify the ways that you can remove these internal barriers to investment by instituting classroom practices that proactively address the root causes of resistance.

Focusing on Your Students

Taking time to understand the root causes of why students resist investing their currencies in the classroom not only provides you with clues that help you figure out how to make learning appealing to students in their own terms, but also allows you to see your students in a new light. And viewing your students from that fresh perspective will help you find ways to establish deeper, more productive learning relationships with them.

Getting to the root of students' resistance can take time. It's best not to settle on one root cause after only a superficial examination. It's important to dig deeply and examine the many layers of their resistance. For instance, some students can feign boredom in order to mask a fear of failure. Other times, students may refuse to access supports not because they are afraid to fail but because they don't trust you. Students' root reasons for resisting investing are layered, and we must tease through those layers first if we hope to choose the right approach to address their resistance. This work requires a methodical approach. You need to identify the reason you *think* a student hasn't invested, then look for the possible hidden reasons *behind* that reason by examining it through the lens of each of the three root causes. As you do so, you will see which of the root causes seems to be exerting the greatest influence.

Take a look at the **Sample Resistance Investigation Worksheet** on page 81. The teacher starts by identifying a fear of failure as the main reason her student, Bob, is resisting investing in her algebra class. Next, she looks to three examples of behavior that have led her to thinking that Bob's root resistance is due to a fear of failure. She thinks through each of these examples and looks for other factors that might explain them. In the end, she identifies solutions informed by both the root cause and the contributing causes that directly address Bob's reasons for resistance.

Now you try it. Think about a particularly resistant student or group of students in your class. Use the **Resistance Investigation Worksheet** on page 82, review the reasons for resisting discussed in this chapter, and identify one or more main reasons your reluctant students may resist investing. Then think through those reasons and attempt to isolate the root causes. Finally, brainstorm a few strategies you might use to help students overcome these resistances. See **Appendix B** for additional guidance on effective instructional responses.

Sample Resistance Analysis Worksheet

Student Name: Bob Marley

The investment I want this student to make: I want Bob to put effort into his homework by following the directions, answering each question in complete sentences, and turning in neat work that is free of careless mistakes by the due date.

This student may resist making this investment because . . . he is afraid of failure.

Because . . . He has already failed algebra once and complains that he has done this work before and didn't get it the first time. He calls my class "stupid" and sits in the back of the class sleeping most of the time. I wonder too if he doesn't see the relevance in the course other than he needs it to graduate. And because he hasn't passed it, graduating has become less important.

Because . . . He resists my efforts to help him. He won't come in after school or during lunch, and if I try to help him in class, he acts like he doesn't care. I wonder if he also doesn't trust me to help? Or is it that he doesn't see how my supports will make a real difference in what he's able to do?

Because . . . He won't answer questions in class anymore after I asked him a question and it was clear that he didn't know some of his basic math facts. The other students teased him that he was stupid, and he shrugged and started "joning" on the other students. It's like he doesn't want them to see that he doesn't understand.

Therefore, I need to . . . Find a way to make failure a natural and inevitable part of my class. Maybe instead of always asking students to supply the right answer, I can do error analysis: give them a wrong answer and ask them to explain why it's wrong. I also need to do more choral responses rather than individual work so that no one sticks out. And maybe I can use growth-oriented feedback as a way of helping Bob figure out how he can get better.

Resistance Analysis Worksheet

Student Name:

The investment I want this student to make:

This student may resist making this investment because . . .

Because . . .

Because . . .

Because . . .

Therefore, I need to . . .

YES, BUT . . .

What if my students are just lazy?

We make a huge leap when we decide that students who do not do their work are just lazy. The same students who sit and do nothing in your classroom expend a great amount of effort doing other things when they're outside the classroom—hanging out with friends, building imaginary worlds, reading graphic novels, exchanging Pokémon cards, playing video games, or perfecting their skateboarding or makeup application skills. What they really are is *efficient,* not lazy. They have chosen to conserve their energy and time and invest it in activities they value more. If you want to overcome "laziness," you have to help students see the value of investing in your classroom. We'll talk about that more in the next chapter.

4

Asking For and Shaping an Investment

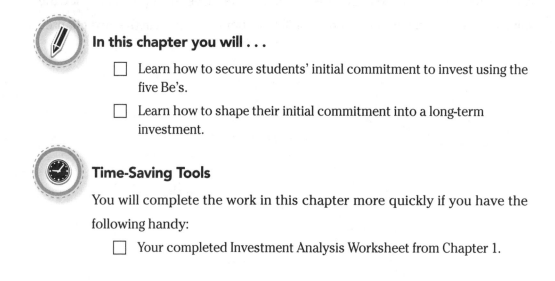

In this chapter you will . . .

- ☐ Learn how to secure students' initial commitment to invest using the five Be's.
- ☐ Learn how to shape their initial commitment into a long-term investment.

Time-Saving Tools

You will complete the work in this chapter more quickly if you have the following handy:

- ☐ Your completed Investment Analysis Worksheet from Chapter 1.

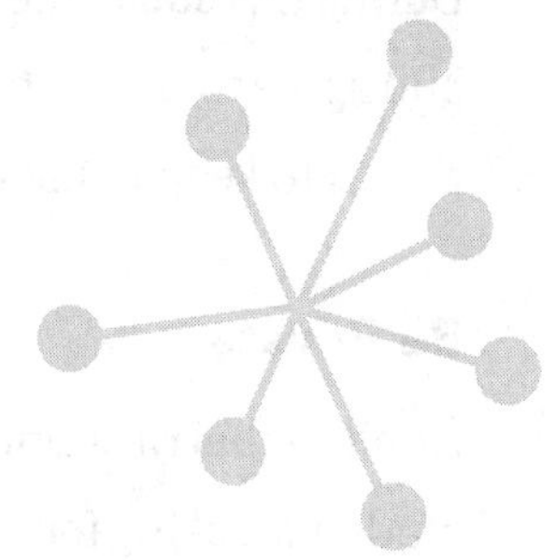

Now that you have selected an investment and addressed potential barriers, you need to get students on board. The next step is to ask students to commit to the investment and guide their first steps toward motivated behavior.

Motivation is a fuzzy concept. We all have different ideas of what motivation is, and often, our idea of motivated behavior differs wildly from our students'. We cannot assume that students will understand intuitively what investments they should be making in the classroom. If you just ask your students to "be motivated" without making it clear what you mean by motivated—what motivation will look like and how they will behave differently when they are motivated—you are leaving their investing to chance. Unless you specifically ask your students to make the investment you're looking for, you're unlikely to get it.

Getting students to invest in your classroom is really a two-step process. First, you must secure an initial commitment to invest, either one-on-one with individual students or with groups of students who are exhibiting the same reluctance to engage. Then, once you have secured the initial investment, you must give students specific direction on the critical next steps they'll need to take in order to successfully invest over the long term. In this chapter, you'll learn how to do both.

Securing the Commitment to Invest

During this stage, the goal is to get students to understand what you're asking of them and agree to do it. That's all. You just want them to make a commitment. Here are five things to keep in mind during this stage of the conversation. I call them the five Be's.

Be Private

Don't embarrass unmotivated students by making your request public. For some students, asking for a private conversation after class might be a good approach; others might find this kind of one-on-one meeting intimidating. Look for opportunities to speak privately with students after class, at your desk quietly while other students are working, at lunch or after school, or even with another trusted adult, such as a parent or counselor. The key is to find a time and a place where students are comfortable and free from public scrutiny.

Be Succinct

Sometimes we shoot ourselves in the foot by using too many words. Students become confused about what we are asking or are so bombarded with choices that they end up making no investment at all. State your request using as few words as possible. You may want your students to make several investments over the course of the year, but focus each request on what you want students to do right now.

Be Positive

Being positive in your request for investment is about shifting students' focus from the negative to the positive. Instead of calling students attention to the "unmotivated behavior" they need to stop ("Stop falling asleep in class" or "You don't turn in your homework"), focus your request on motivated behavior you want them to start ("Stay awake the entire period" or "Turn in completed homework on time").

Be Specific

Often, our requests are too vague. Use very precise words to ask students for the investment you desire. Think about the work you did in Chapter 1 to refine your target investment; use this as a starting point to narrate for students the kinds of behaviors you want to see. Rather than say to a student that you want her to start paying better attention, for example, ask her to take notes, keep her head off the desk, track you with her eyes as you teach, and ask questions related to the class discussion. Focus on what the student can do right now to succeed from this point forward.

Be Quiet

After you ask for an investment, be quiet. Don't explain your reasons for asking. Stop talking and wait. Let the student speak next. Even if it takes 10 minutes, be quiet and wait patiently for the student to agree. Many reluctant or resistant students have gotten very good at waiting you out. You have to demonstrate to them that you are willing to wait for the commitment you want.

Sometimes students are silent because they need time to process what you are asking them to do and figure out if and how they will do it. Don't interrupt their internal dialogue. Being silent gives them the time they need to make their commitment.

If, during the conversation, you have any doubts that a student is not actually committing to the investment, try this conversation again at a different time. This might take a couple of days or even a couple of weeks. Don't rush it or try to force it. Unless students make an initial commitment to invest, they will not take the next steps they need to invest successfully.

THINK ABOUT . . .

Focus on one reluctant learner in your class. How might he or she respond to this conversation? What preparation could you do ahead of time to help ensure that this conversation will actually lead to a commitment to invest?

Shaping the Investment

Once you have secured the initial commitment to invest, take a few additional steps to help shape that investment to support long-term success. This means clarifying to students what successful investment really looks like and how they can do it.

Help Students Set Goals

One of the best ways to help students invest successfully is to involve them in setting their own investment-related goals. When students are involved in setting their own goals for their learning, not only do they learn more, but their motivation to accomplish these goals increases, as does their ability to self-evaluate and self-regulate their participation and performance in the classroom (Saphier & Gower, 1997). Goal setting—and tracking progress toward those goals—makes the idea of successful investment more tangible. Here are some guidelines to follow:

- ***Make the goals specific.*** Specific goals are measurable and contain criteria for effective performance. Goals focused on the speed, quality, or quantity of work tend to work better than more amorphous commitments. Help students commit to doing their work within a particular amount of time, or commit to completing a certain amount of work, or improving in a particular skill or currency. For instance, students can set goals for completing a certain number of problems within a set period of time, reading a certain number of chapters for homework, or reducing the number of spelling and punctuation errors in their next paper.
- ***Make the goals challenging but attainable.*** Goals that are too easy are boring and can actually be demotivating to students. The more difficult the goal, the more effort students will expend to achieve it—but only as long as they see the goal as doable. Work with students to set goals within, but at the outer edge of, their ability.
- ***Make the goals short-term rather than long-term.*** Setting up short-term goals is less likely to overwhelm students, especially those who are initially resistant. It also allows you to go for the "quick win," which helps build momentum. Students need to see that success is within their reach and that being successful feels good; once they have a taste for it, they'll want more. As their degree of investment in the classroom increases, you can move them toward more long-term goals, but even these should be broken up into smaller goals so that payoffs are frequent and regular.
- ***Try visually tracking students' progress.*** Using graphic illustrations, such as line or bar graphs, shows students how their incremental successes are moving them toward a much bigger goal.

Show Students How to Invest Successfully

Most kids, if asked, will tell you that they want to do well in school. Disengaged students' problem isn't necessarily that they don't *want* to do well but that they don't know *how* to do well. Teachers can sometimes exacerbate the problem by sending students mixed messages. We tell them that they should just try, implying that effort is the key to success. But we know ourselves that this isn't necessarily true, and students who try their best and still don't see a payoff eventually realize it for themselves and just give up. We can get much better results by giving our students a clearly mapped path to success.

I remember learning this lesson for myself. I used to get so frustrated when the majority of my students would regularly miss the deadlines I'd set for finishing an assigned novel. Why were they so unmotivated? Then one day, it finally occurred to me that all these "unmotivated" readers had started the novel; they just hadn't finished it. Maybe it wasn't that they weren't willing to make this investment but that they didn't really understand how to invest successfully.

When I assigned the next novel, I asked my students to read the first three pages in class and to time themselves to see how long it took. When everyone had finished and recorded their time, I asked them to divide their time by three (the number of pages they'd read) and then multiply that number by 257 (the number of pages in the novel). Their final answer, I explained, represented approximately how much time it would take for them to finish the novel.

At my direction, the students went on to take out their planners and schedule reading time over the next two weeks. I challenged them to figure out how would they find the 6 or 8 or 10 hours it would take them to finish the novel by the due date. When the due date arrived, all but three students had finished the novel, and these three admitted that they hadn't stuck to their schedule.

What was the reason for this dramatic change? Was it because more of my students were properly motivated this time around? No. It was because I had asked them for the right investment in the right way. I got them to commit to reading the novel *and* I showed them how to do it. Instead of giving them vague direction to finish the novel, I helped them understand the investment of time it would take to meet the deadline and then helped them figure out how they would make the investment.

The lesson here is that once you've secured students' initial agreement to invest, you must immediately begin to show them how to invest successfully. It isn't enough to identify the endpoint—the ultimate investments you want your students to make; you also need to think about what the pathway to high motivation might look like to your students. Here are two important pieces of guidance:

- ***Always identify and communicate the investment's first step.*** Say that you've secured students' commitment to pay attention during your lectures. What are the critical behaviors students need to implement immediately? Do you want them to take notes on the lecture? Do you want them to stop interrupting others during your lecture? Do you want them to just stay awake? What is the one thing students can do to dramatically alter their investment in your lecture? Once you've decided what the first step of the investment is, communicate it clearly. It's not enough for you to know what you want to see; students need to know this, too—in very explicit terms.

- ***Be sure to provide the tools necessary to complete the first step's critical activities.*** If you want them to take notes during class, show them how. If you want them to stop interrupting, tell them what they should be doing instead. If you want them to stay awake, give them strategies for doing so. Showing students *how* to meet the demands of the investment you are asking of them is the way to ensure they can fulfill their commitment.

THINK ABOUT . . .

How does the way that you ask students to invest affect their willingness or ability to commit to investing?

YOUR TURN

Acquire: Think about your target investment, and think about the steps students will need to take to successfully make that investment in your classroom.

Apply: Take a look at the way that you currently ask students to invest in your classroom. Use the five Be's to reshape your requests.

Assimilate: Think about the current ways that you help students invest successfully. What might you do to increase their likelihood of committing? Identify ways that you can build value across the year so that students can see the cumulative value of their long-term investment.

Adapt: Identify ways you can indirectly ask students to invest in your classroom while still being true to the five Be's.

Focusing Your Efforts

Now that you've considered the guidelines for asking for and securing a commitment to invest, go ahead and apply them to your target investment, using the **Investment Request and Planning Worksheet** on page 91. This template can be used to plan your pitch to individual students or groups of students.

Investment Request and Planning Worksheet

Target Investment:	
Secure the Commitment	
Be Private Identify where and when you will hold this conversation to ensure students' privacy.	
Be Succinct Phrase your request for commitment in the fewest words possible. Try to stick to one to two sentences.	
Be Positive Refine your request to make sure you're using positive terms.	
Be Specific Refine your request to be specific.	
Shape the Investment	
Goals What goals can you and your students set, and how will you track these goals?	
Steps for Success What steps can students take in order to invest successfully?	

YES, BUT . . .

What if my students still *won't make the investment I want?*

If you have gone through the steps outlined in this book to help students invest in your classroom and your students still won't make a commitment, here are three steps you can take:

- ***Make sure that you have removed all unintentional barriers to successful investment.*** I know that you spent time thinking about this in Chapter 2, but give it another look. Is there something you overlooked? Is there something that you didn't consider a barrier that might be getting in students' way? Double-check to ensure that you have removed all barriers to investing.
- ***Enlist the help of other trusted adults.*** Whom does your resistant student trust? Can a parent, guardian, guidance counselor, administrator, teaching aide, security guard, maintenance person, or fellow teacher help you work with your student? Look for an adult the student trusts and enlist that person's help in securing the commitment from your student.
- ***Look for bright spots and study the areas where students are investing already.*** Try to find out what students are investing in both in and outside school, and determine, if you can, why they are investing in those places. Is the student doing the work for another teacher because that teacher works with them after school or has built a rapport with the student? Do you need to do the same before asking for an investment? Is the student invested in a particular video game or book series at home? Can you talk to the student to discover what is so appealing about the video game or book and how you can use those elements in your own classroom? Study the investments your students are currently making. They may hold clues for how you can secure a similar investment from your students.

5

Putting It All Together

In this chapter you will . . .

- ☐ Use what you have learned throughout this guide to develop a comprehensive plan for motivating your students.
- ☐ Learn strategies for helping students sustain their investment over time.

Time-Saving Tools

You will complete the work in this chapter more quickly if you have the following handy:

- ☐ Your completed worksheets from Chapters 1, 2, 3, and 4.

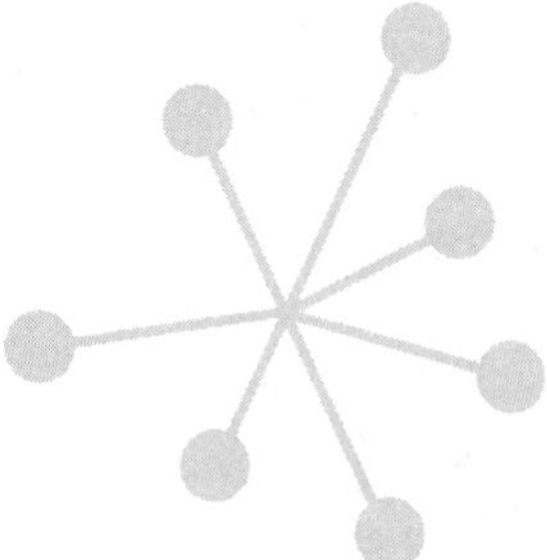

You've thought through each of the steps for helping students invest in your classroom. Now it's time to put everything together and launch your new approach to motivating reluctant learners.

We have looked at the various stages of an approach to motivation based on starting where your students are. Considered together, they provide the structure for a comprehensive motivation plan.

Developing Your Motivation Plan

Before we begin, let's review the stages in the process.

TAKE IT STEP BY STEP

How to Motivate Reluctant Learners

1. Choose the right investments.
2. Create a classroom worth investing in.
3. Understand and address students' resistance.
4. Ask for and shape a commitment to invest.

Step 1: Choose the Right Investments

Motivation is ultimately an investment decision. Before you can ask students to invest in your classroom, you must first identify the specific investments you want them to make. Begin by examining your own concept of motivation, and then use that as a starting point for shaping the specific investments you want your students to make. Then use the SMORES criteria—*Specific, Meaningful, Observable, Realistic,* worth the *Effort,* and *Small*—to refine each investment you want students to make in the classroom.

Step 2: Create a Classroom Worth Investing In

After identifying the investments you want students to make in your classroom, the next step is to look at your classroom and make sure that it doesn't present unintentional barriers to investing. Then you can begin to build classroom structures that promote autonomy, mastery, purpose, and belonging. By addressing these fundamental needs, you can make your classroom a place where students will be more willing to engage.

Step 3: Understand and Address Students' Resistance

In addition to addressing the external factors that may be decreasing student motivation, it is important to identify and address students' internal reasons for not investing in the classroom. Think about your students and the reasons they choose not to engage, and then address these reasons—on their terms.

Step 4: Ask for and Shape the Investment

The most critical step in this process is to get students to actually make an investment. You will improve the odds that students will commit to new, motivated behavior by shaping your shape your request according to the five Be's: *be succinct, be specific, be positive, be private,* and *be quiet.* Using these strategies, you can ask students for the right investment and then work with them to develop a plan for taking the first steps.

Assembling Your Plan

The **Motivation Plan Template** on pages 96–97 will help you turn all the work you've done so far on this guide's worksheets into a comprehensive plan to motivate reluctant learners to invest in your classroom. As you implement your plan, use the **Motivation Checklist** on page 98 to ensure you're attending to this approach's critical features. **Appendix C** provides a complete example of a motivation plan.

Motivation Plan Template

Target Investment What investment do you want students to make? (Use the *Investment Analysis Worksheet* on pages 33–34 to phrase the investment in specific terms.)	
Why are you asking students to make this investment? How is this investment meaningful? (Use the *Investment Analysis Worksheet* on pages 33–34 to identify how the investment will be meaningful and worthwhile for students.)	
What **classroom barriers** do you believe are preventing your students from making this investment? (Use the *Classroom Barrier Anticipation Worksheet* on page 45 to identify potential classroom barriers.)	
How will you remove these classroom barriers to investing? (Use the *Classroom Barrier Anticipation Worksheet* on page 45 and the *Classroom Climate Worksheet* on page 63 to identify possible solutions.)	

Motivation Plan Template (cont.)

What **internal barriers** to making this investment do you believe your students may have? (Use the *Resistance Analysis Worksheet* on page 82 to identify specific internal barriers.)	
How will you address these reasons for resisting? (Use the *Resistance Analysis Worksheet* on page 82 to identify possible solutions.)	
How will you phrase your commitment request and help students invest successfully? (Use the *Investment Request and Planning Worksheet* on page 91 to identify how you will ask for and help students commit to investing in your classroom.)	

Motivation Checklist

Build a Classroom Worth Investing In

- ☐ I have created a classroom that is most conducive to the way my students learn best.
- ☐ I am clear about what currencies the lesson demands.
- ☐ I have made sure that the lesson does not privilege my currencies as the only acceptable forms of currency.
- ☐ I have worked out ways to make explicit the currencies required by the lesson.
- ☐ I have examined my classroom to make sure that I am not unintentionally creating barriers to investing.
- ☐ I have removed all classroom barriers to investing.
- ☐ I am helping students who do not have the required currencies or a viable alternative acquire the currencies they need.
- ☐ I have built in classroom structures that offer students autonomy of task, time, team, and technique.
- ☐ I have built in classroom structures that offer students mastery.
- ☐ I have built in classroom structures that offer students a sense of purpose.
- ☐ I have built in classroom structures that foster a sense of belonging.

Uncover and Address the Reasons Students Resist

- ☐ I have identified students' reason(s) for resisting investing.
- ☐ I have addressed students' fear of failure by including specific strategies to build students' resilience.
- ☐ I have addressed a lack of relevance for students by personalizing content.
- ☐ I have addressed students' lack of trust by deliberately building relationships with students.
- ☐ I have looked for ways to demonstrate value on students' terms rather than my own terms.

Ask For the Investment

- ☐ I have clearly defined the long-term investment goal.
- ☐ I have asked for an investment that is directly connected to the goal.
- ☐ I have asked for a specific investment.
- ☐ I have proposed the highest realistic investment students can make at the time.
- ☐ I have proposed a meaningful investment.
- ☐ I have helped students set specific goals.
- ☐ I have asked these students to make an investment.
- ☐ I have held these students accountable to their investment.
- ☐ I look for ways to help my students continue to invest in the classroom using their new currencies.

Sustaining Motivation over Time

Motivation isn't a single decision students make once and for all; it's a decision that they must make day after day. Securing an initial investment is a good start, but if you want to sustain students' motivation over time, there are several things to do.

Build Habits, Routines, and Rituals

How do you save for retirement? While some of us regularly study the stock market and earnings reports, run the numbers ourselves, and call a broker to initiate trades, most of us have funds withdrawn automatically from our accounts each month and invested for us in a mutual fund or annuity. Why? Because it's easy. We can set our investing on automatic pilot and not have to think about it.

Habits, routines, and rituals are a great way to make investing automatic for students. They don't have to go through the entire decision-making process every time they face an investment decision. They simply act, because they've become accustomed to doing so. If you think about it, our classrooms are filled with routines. If students are used to coming into class and chatting for 10 minutes before getting to work, it's a habit and a routine, even though it isn't a beneficial one. To get and sustain better behavior from students, you have to help them build a better habit. This is a three-step process.

- ***Identify your goal.*** Do you want your students to complete their homework each night? Do you want your students to come to class on time and ready to work each day? Do you want your students to treat each other kindly? Do you want your students to stay focused during their seatwork? Decide what behaviors and investments you want your students to make in the classroom.
- ***Determine what routines or rituals will help students make this investment a habit.*** For example, if you want your students to complete their homework each night, you might require them to write down their assignment in the same place and get them to set aside a specific time and place for completing homework. If you want students to be ready to work at the bell, you might consistently provide work for them to do during this time by instituting opening activities. If you want them to treat each other more kindly, you might post classroom "rules of engagement" and model how to interact in a considerate and positive way. If you want them to maintain focus during their seatwork, you might establish clear routines for completing it and classroom rituals that celebrate its completion. When planning your approach, pick habits and routines that are consistent with your students' currencies and easy to embrace.

Your students are likely to resist a routine that calls for them to work quietly in their seats for 90 minutes at a stretch, no matter how much you reinforce it.

- ***Introduce the routines and give students plenty of practice.*** If you want your students to come into the classroom in a certain way, take them into the hall and practice it. If you want to build a routine, explain the routine and practice it. You might also want to create a few action triggers that remind students to act. For instance, you could start every class by reading a poem as a way of helping students settle down and focus. You might use a call-and-response chant or handclaps to signal to students that you need their attention. You might tell students to do their homework after they have had their last meal for the day as a way of getting them to connect doing homework with something they do at home each night. You might color-code your handouts so that students know automatically to put the yellow sheets in their folders, put the blue sheets in their notebooks, and use the pink sheets to study for tests. Triggers like these make investing easier. They remind students of the investment they should be making and help them invest automatically and consistently.

Acknowledge Incremental Growth

It is unrealistic to expect resistant students to immediately become invested in every aspect of your classroom every day. Even when they begin to invest, they still might skip an occasional class, put their heads on the desk once in a while, leave an assignment unfinished, or give in to distracting behavior during a lesson. If you want to help unmotivated students sustain motivation over time, you need to praise incremental growth.

Reinforce each step students take toward behaving in motivated ways. If they never turn in homework and one day come to class with 5 out of 25 problems done, don't complain about the 20 problems they haven't done; acknowledge the 5 they completed. It's progress.

Learning to spot and reinforce steps toward improvement can be tough for us. We want perfect performance every time, and accepting anything less may feel like lowering our standards. After all, 5 out of 25 is still a failing grade. But if we want students to take more than one step toward success, we have to acknowledge that first step. Rather than bemoan the fact that the student completed only five problems, say, "Good for you for taking the first step! If you can complete the first five problems, I know you can do the rest." Withholding notice and praise until you get perfect performance is one of the best ways to kill motivation; acknowledging incremental steps is one of the best ways to nurture it.

Focus on What's Working

Motivating students isn't an event; it's a process. It's a series of steps in the right direction that eventually lead to "unmotivated" students acting like motivated students.

Thus, early in the process, it may seem that you are putting in a lot of effort for very few results. You are working hard to adjust your classroom so that it is worth investing in, you are removing barriers to investing, you are uncovering and addressing students' reasons for not investing, and you are securing (you think) students' commitment to invest. And then the students turn in 5 of 25 homework problems.

The funny thing about change, though, is that it starts small and then builds. Once students take that first step toward investing, the others are so much easier—particularly if you're there to provide support and reinforcement. Whatever you do, don't give up. Things will likely move slowly at first, but over time, you'll see students making bigger and bigger investments in the classroom.

As momentum for investment builds, instead of lamenting what's not going as well as you'd like, consider what's working and how you can replicate and scale it. When you see a reluctant student make a choice to invest even a little bit, pay attention. Ask yourself: *What circumstances or strategies seemed to have enticed him to learn? What topic or subject or activity sparked her to try? What currencies does he seem most comfortable using? What values seem most motivating to her?*

Remember, no student is unmotivated all the time. Look for the times when your resistant students do choose to participate, to do their work, to give your or even another teacher's class a chance and study. Doing so will not only give you clues about how to best work with a student, it will also reassure you that you can make a difference and that it is possible to help a student make the choice to invest in class.

Some Final Words About Rewards

We've all used rewards at some time or another. Whether you give students a homework pass or bonus points or additional recess time or a piece of candy, rewards are a dependable tool to use in motivation efforts, and that's because rewards work. Many students will work for a reward when they won't work for anything else.

The main problem with using rewards comes from relying on them exclusively. Rewards don't foster an intrinsic motivation to learn; they simply promote an external motivation to earn the reward. Bob Sullo (2009) puts it this way: "What makes the use of external rewards for learning so insidious is that when we provide external, tangible rewards to students, we inadvertently devalue education and learning. The unintentional but powerful message we provide students is this: "What we are asking you to do is not inherently valuable. It is worth the effort only because if you do what we ask, you will get something valuable" (p. 32).

Another concern is that motivation through rewards places the control in the teacher's hands. The teacher identifies the appropriate behavior, the teacher selects the reward, and the teacher determines when the student is worthy of receiving the reward. We have already discussed that a critical element of motivation is a sense of autonomy and control, but that sense of autonomy and control is something most reward systems unintentionally undermine.

Using Rewards Wisely

Ultimately, rewards can damage motivation rather than encourage it. In fact, the only time rewards seem to work without harmful side effects is when you are rewarding students for completing routine tasks—memorizing material, cleaning the boards, keeping their desks neat, or walking quietly through the halls. Even then, you must be careful in how you reward students so that you don't get them focused on the reward rather than on completing the task. Dan Pink (2009) offers these suggestions for using rewards wisely:

- Rewards should be unexpected and offered only after the task is complete.
- Shift from "if/then" rewards ("If the entire class works quietly, then you will earn 10 minutes of extra recess") to "now that" rewards ("Congratulations! Everyone was in their seats and ready to work by the time the late bell rang. We'll celebrate with five minutes of free time at the end of the period").
- Supplement rewards for completing routine tasks by offering a rationale for why the task is necessary, acknowledging that the task is boring, and allowing students to complete the task in their own way.

Shifting Students to a New Kind of Reward System

Despite the ineffectiveness of a rewards-only motivation system, many of our students expect to be rewarded for their efforts. So how do we wean them off these external rewards and help them see and value the internal rewards inherent in learning? We show students how to create their own rewards.

Showing students how to create their own rewards starts with giving growth-oriented feedback and affirmation that will help them "own" their learning experiences. When students attempt work, give them feedback early in the process that shows them how they can be more successful, how they can turn their mistakes into successes, and how through their own efforts, they have improved their learning. Instead of rewarding them for a job well done, celebrate their success. Thus, rather than promise a movie *if* students complete their work, celebrate the fact that students have completed their work once it is done. You might say, "I am so proud of how hard you worked to complete this assignment. Look at all the new strategies you have learned! I just know you feel smarter. How shall we celebrate your accomplishment?" Then allow students a choice of currency-linked activities, such as time to read a book of their choice, the opportunity to do their classwork outside in the school courtyard, or a congratulatory postcard home to their parents. I even saw one teacher set up a gong in her classroom so that students could ring it when they accomplished a really tough learning goal. Other teachers have created "Learning Rock Star" pins for students to wear when they have worked hard and learned something new. I've even heard of teachers setting up periodic "graduation ceremonies" throughout the year as students move from reading at one grade level to the next. Focusing on celebrations rather than if/then rewards helps students feel the emotional payoff for their learning and make them less dependent on rewards for their motivation.

YES, BUT . . .

What about intrinsic motivation?

Most of us don't do everything we do for intrinsic reasons. We work at least partially for a paycheck. We drive the speed limit not because we enjoy driving 25 miles per hour when we are in a hurry but because we don't want to get a ticket and imperil the lives of the other drivers around us. We work weekends in order to meet deadlines and complete paperwork because those tasks are part of our job. We clean behind the fridge because company is coming over, and we endure family dinners with our kooky Aunt Midge so we don't upset our mothers. In fact, very little of what we do is purely intrinsically motivated.

The same is true of our students. They may never love literature the way that we do. They may never get their kicks from solving impossible math problems, and spelling may never be as important to them as it is to us. But that doesn't mean that they can't enjoy these activities. If we can help students see the value in reading literature or solving impossible math problems or spelling, and if we can demonstrate that value *in their terms,* we can help them choose to invest their time and energy in these activities, even if they aren't intrinsically motivated to do so. For many of our students, intrinsic motivation has to be developed. It comes only after they have experienced the pleasure of doing well and know the reward for success. We can teach students to develop intrinsic motivation, but it is unfair to expect them to be intrinsically motivated from the start.

Conclusion

Ultimately, motivating unmotivated students starts with a relationship. Currencies and investing are just a way of conceptualizing that relationship and helping us understand that what happens between us and our students is transactional; we give and we get. When we see our relationship with students in this way, we can understand that any breakdown in the relationship is a really breakdown in the transaction. We have to fix the elements of that transaction if we are going to repair the relationship.

Some of you may bristle at my describing the relationship between teachers and students using language usually associated with the marketplace. You may even feel that seeing motivation as an investment decision commoditizes learning in some way. These reservations are understandable, but the truth is, all relationships are transactional. In healthy relationships, the transaction is mutually beneficial. In dysfunctional ones, the transaction is one-sided or mutually destructive. Even in the most altruistic of exchanges, the giver gets something out of it—often just the joy of serving others. What we give and what we get drive all human interactions. If you can accept this view of your classroom, it will open up an array of possible ways to meet your students' needs.

An approach to motivation based on helping students invest their currencies in the classroom does serve an altruistic purpose. It helps you truly start where your students are, rather than where you think they ought to be. It communicates to students that it's OK for them to be exactly who they are, while also showing them opportunities to grow and become better or more expanded versions of themselves. It helps students learn to love learning on their own terms. Rather than participate in class, try hard, complete assignments, and challenge themselves because you tell them to, they get to the point where they do these things because doing them is personally important to them.

As you embark on this approach to motivation, here are a few key points to keep in mind:

- ***Don't rush it.*** Helping disengaged learners invest in the classroom takes time. You cannot expect students to turn around completely on day one. Instead, keep investing in them. Pay attention to their currencies, and find ways to connect and integrate their currencies into both your curriculum and your classroom environment. Eventually, students will begin to come around.
- ***Build tolerance for risk over time.*** Asking students to invest in the classroom involves a degree of risk on their part. Risk tolerance is like a muscle that gets stronger with regular exercise. Build a series of smaller risks, and help students navigate these risks successfully before asking them to take on bigger ones.
- ***Remember, you cannot control students.*** Effective motivation is not about getting students to do what you want them to do. That's manipulation. Effective motivation is about helping students understand the value of school in terms that matter to them. Then students are free to make the choice of whether or not they want to invest. It is *their* decision.
- ***Motivation is not compliance.*** Many students comply with rules and procedures not because they are motivated but because it's easier for them to comply than to refuse or because they are afraid of the consequences otherwise. In a very real sense, these students are also reluctant learners. Look past compliance for signs that students are making an investment—no matter how small—in your classroom and in their own learning. If you can't find this evidence, take action.
- ***Don't forget the emotional side of motivation.*** Often, we attempt to convince students to invest in our classroom by making a logical case, but the decision to invest is not purely logical. We also have to address the emotional payoff of the investment. Don't just demonstrate value in terms of what investing in their learning will do for students; remember to also demonstrate value in terms of how it will make students feel.
- ***Be careful not to resort to fear tactics.*** Many of our attempts to motivate students in school are based in fear. We tell them that if they don't learn this now, they

will have a tougher time in middle school, or they will fail the class and have to go to summer school, or they won't get into a good college. Although these warnings may be true, fear is a poor motivator and can end up paralyzing students. Hope, on the other hand, is a very powerful motivator. Students need you to give them hope that they *can* do what you're asking them to do, and they need you to show them how making an investment will lead to rich payoffs that will matter to them.

- ***This is a highly nuanced process.*** Although this guide lays out a set of steps, how you engage in each of those steps will depend on who you are, your teaching or leadership context, and most important, the needs of your students. Think through each step of this process and adapt the steps as needed.

Showing students how to take their currencies—their interests, abilities, experiences, preferences, talents, and everything else that makes them who they are—and invest them in the classroom is the key to motivating them and keeping them motivated over time. It means building classrooms where students feel safe being who they are. And it means recognizing and taking advantage of opportunities within and beyond the curriculum, to help students learn in ways that work best for them. When you do, you make it possible for reluctant and resistant students to rewrite their legacies of failure and disengagement and become motivated to change their relationship to school, with you, and with learning.

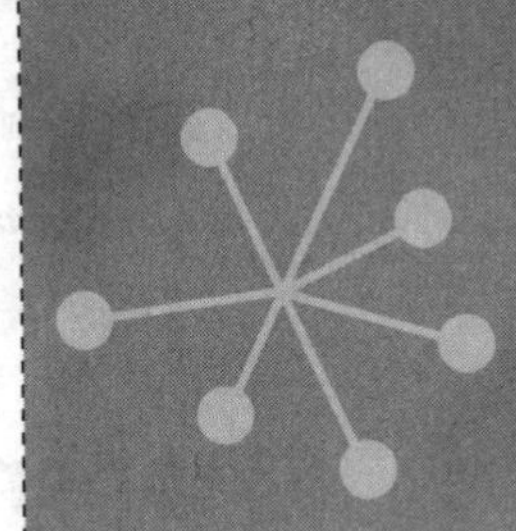

Appendixes

Appendix A: A General List of Currencies

Knowledge	Soft Skills
Academic vocabulary Academic background knowledge Common sense Knowledge about an outside area of interest Cultural literacy	Study skills Effective note-taking skills Ability to navigate the school system Ability to recognize when he/she needs help Ability to contribute to group discussions Ability to manage his/her own behavior in a classroom Ability to sustain attention Ability to set and manage long-term goals Ability to read and take notes from a text Ability to figure out a problem using a systematic approach Effective listening skills
Social Skills	**Network Affiliations**
Ability to make and keep friends Ability to get others to help Ability to enter and participate in conversations with others Ability to work cooperatively with others Leadership abilities Ability to interact comfortably with classmates who are not personal friends Ability to interact comfortably with adults Ability to read a social situation and produce the appropriate behavior An understanding of cultural norms Effective listening skills	Availability of an adult support network Friends within the classroom Membership in a community group Membership in a faith-based community Membership in an academically oriented club or network

Appendix B: Instructional Strategies to Address the Root Causes of Resistance

Fear of Failure

Ask for choral responses. Reduce the threat of students' appearing foolish by using choral responses during class discussions. Rather than ask individual students to respond to your questions, ask the entire class to respond in unison. Have the class repeat the response several times. In that way, even if a student didn't know the answer the first time, the student can learn from his/her peers and have a chance to get the answer right.

Use cooperative pairs. This strategy is designed for classwork consisting of problems sets or other worksheet-based, numbered activities. Pair students into teams of two and distribute the assignment. Ask them to circle a certain number of random items on the worksheet (for instance, a student might circle numbers 1, 4, 7, and 10). Have students complete their work individually. When they get to a circled item, they must stop and compare their answers with their partners—and they must not continue to the next problem until they agree on an answer. With this approach, students who are afraid that they do not have the right answer have a chance to confer with a classmate before turning in their work. The discussion requirement nudges them to support their answers and gives them the opportunity to learn from one another.

Use numbered heads. Divide students into teams of two (designating one as "Number One" and the other as "Letter A" to discourage the impression of a hierarchy). Have students work individually on an assignment. When work is complete, ask team members to trade papers, and go through each answer as a whole class. Ask students to raise their hand if they have an answer different from the correct answer. Because they are looking at their partner's papers, they are more likely to raise their hand (because they don't have to admit their own failure), and you are more likely to get an accurate assessment of classwide understanding. Have the students share with you the answer they have in front of them and write the answer on the board. Then take the wrong answer and show students how to turn it into a right answer.

Have students assume roles for discussion. Many students are afraid to express their ideas during a class discussion because they are afraid of being wrong. If this is the case with your students, assign a specific role for them to play during the discussion. For example, ask them to pretend that they are particular characters in an assigned story or certain historical figures associated with an event being studied. Ask them to argue the point from the perspective of a particular stakeholder or from a certain school of thought. In this way, students who are afraid to express their own ideas can participate in the discussion, because any ideas they express are technically not their own.

Use error analysis. This strategy is designed to help students learn to work their way out of failure. Take student errors or common errors and, as a class, try to figure out what the root error is and how to fix it. You can also pass out an assignment that is already completed and have students find the errors. For instance, provide a set of 10 math problems that have already been solved, telling students that 4 of the problems are correct and 6 are incorrect. Ask them to identify the correct problems. Next, have them identify the key error in the 6 incorrect problems and fix that error to turn the incorrect answers into correct answers.

Use conditional retakes. Allow students to retake assessments and resubmit assignments on the condition that they engage in some corrective action before the retake. This might consist of a review of supplementary material; an error analysis of their first assessment/assignment; or additional tutoring, coaching, or instruction.

Lack of Relevance

Use advance organizers. Advance organizers help students see how all the parts of the unit are connected. Distribute an organizer at the beginning of each unit of instruction, and refer to it often during the course of the unit so that students can see how each assignment connects to the unit's overall objectives. (For more on advance organizers, including an advance organizer template, see the *How to Plan Rigorous Instruction* guide in this series.)

Choose culturally relevant materials. Not every assignment, reading, or project has to have cultural relevance, but including culturally relevant materials significantly boosts students' connection to and engagement with content. Select literature and texts across multiple genres and perspectives, making certain to reflect the diversity of the classroom population so that students have a chance to "see" themselves and their cultures in material they're studying. Encourage a community of learners by helping organize book clubs or literature circles, and use cooperative learning strategies such as Jigsaw. Use role-playing strategies and provide various options for completing an assignment. When possible, allow students to set their own goals for a project and to select their own reading materials.

Create study groups. Even when the work itself seems irrelevant, students who must work together toward the same goal tend to find relevance in the group even when they cannot see it in the work. Have students form study groups to work together toward specific instructional goals. Provide structure for each group by defining group roles, providing group materials and schedules, and helping each group identify clear group goals. For more on forming study groups, visit www.mindstepsinc.com/motivation.

Demystify soft skills. Many students have difficulty seeing how their currencies are a match for the demands of the classroom. For each assignment, explain what soft-skill currencies will be required, how they can be used, and how they will help students successfully complete the assignment. In doing so, you help students understand how the currencies they have already may be a match for the assignment, and if students don't have the required currencies, they can learn from your explanation how to go about developing those currencies or know to ask for additional help if they feel they cannot develop these soft skills on their own.

Build background knowledge. Use minilessons to accelerate students' background knowledge so that they are able to connect what they are learning to what they know already. Two days before students will need the background knowledge, open the class with an appropriate short lesson, reading, or video clip. Then, one day before they will need the background knowledge, conduct a brief discussion to make sure that students understand the information and have had a chance to digest it. On the day students will need to use the background knowledge, begin the class by reminding students of what they have learned. When you introduce the new material, make sure to draw a clear connection to this reviewed background knowledge.

Use the statement strategy. To build interest in an upcoming unit and help students see the relevance of a new topic, develop five to seven statements about the topic addressing central themes, important points, and common misconceptions. Phrase the statements ambiguously so that they can each be taken more than one way. Then, present the statements to students at the beginning the unit's first lesson, asking students to agree or disagree with each. Once students have agreed or disagreed with each statement individually, conduct a class discussion in which they must defend their answers. Do not designate answers right or wrong. Simply facilitate the discussion and make sure that both sides are heard. Then, throughout the unit, return to those statements and ask students if they *still* agree or disagree with each one. As students learn more about the topic, they will build relevance by comparing what they are learning with their original ideas.

Use anticipation guides for texts. This strategy helps students think about how the text is relevant to their own opinions, ideas, and beliefs. Before asking students to read a text, create an anticipation guide with 7 to 10 statements, opinions, and controversial ideas students will encounter in the text. Ask students to work individually or in pairs to read each statement and then respond by agreeing, disagreeing, or qualifying each statement. Discuss students' responses as a class. Then have students read the text, noting whether the author agrees, disagrees, or qualifies each statement, and compare their own responses to those of the authors. Where do they agree with the author? Where do they disagree? Finally, ask students whether the author persuaded them to change their answers, and why or why not.

Lack of Trust

Use proactive intervention. Proactive intervention puts supports into place before students need them. Rather than wait for students to fail and try to provide supports on the fly, plan supports ahead of time and communicate your support plan to students and to parents. For detailed instructions on how to create proactive intervention plans, see the *How to Support Struggling Students* guide in this series, and visit www.mindstepsinc.com/support for support plan templates.

Praise effort, not ability. Many students don't trust their teachers because they fear that their teachers are interested in judging them as smart or not smart, capable or incapable. Instead of praising ability, praise individual effort. Provide specific praise for what students are doing to grow, and avoid evaluative comments.

Collect and respond to feedback. Students will trust you more if they see that you genuinely want their input and will respond to their needs. Periodically give students an anonymous, paper-and-pencil survey that rates how well you are supporting them and helping them learn. (Alternatively, take your class to the computer lab and have them complete a survey online, using one of the free survey services available. These services will tally responses for you.) After you collect the feedback and analyze it, take a few minutes during class to provide "feedback on feedback," talking about the trends you noticed in the survey data and discussing how you will respond to students' needs based on their survey responses. Then, make a concerted effort to make appropriate adjustments to your classroom to accommodate student feedback.

Explain classroom policies. Often, students will trust you more if you help them understand why certain classroom policies and procedures are in place. Give students your reasons for policies and procedures. Even if they disagree with your rationale, they can at least understand where you are coming from, and that engenders a degree of trust.

Appendix C: Sample Motivation Plan

Target Investment What investment do you want students to make? (Use the *Investment Analysis Worksheet* on pages 33–34 to phrase the target investment in specific terms.)	I would like my students to complete their math homework each night according to the directions, following all the steps, showing all their work, and submitting it on time.
Why are you asking students to make this investment? How is this investment meaningful? (Use the *Investment Analysis Worksheet* on pages 33–34 to identify how the investment will be meaningful and worthwhile for students.)	The homework assignments give students practice on the skills we are learning in class each day. Without this practice, students will not be ready for the next level, since each skill builds on the prior skill.
What **classroom barriers** do you believe are preventing your students from making this investment? (Use the *Classroom Barrier Anticipation Worksheet* on page 45 to identify potential classroom barriers.)	Barrier #1: Many students do not have anyone at home who will remind them to complete their homework or reinforce homework time. Barrier #2: Many students do not have parental support or help at home and may get stuck with the academic component of the work. Barrier #3: Some students may need more autonomy and choice as to what problems to do. Some of the problems seem too easy or hard for them to complete on their own.
How will you remove these classroom barriers to investing? (Use the *Classroom Barrier Anticipation Worksheet* on page 45 and the *Classroom Climate Worksheet* on page 63 to identify possible solutions.)	For Barrier #1 (lack of homework reminders/reinforcement): I can form a homework buddy system so that these students can help each other. (TEAM and BELONGING) For Barrier #2 (lack of academic support): I can give students a "break glass" strategy to use when they get stuck, or they can call their homework buddies and work together. (TEAM and MASTERY) For Barrier #3 (need for greater autonomy and more choice): I can create more tiered assignments to help students have some choice and still get the practice they need. (MASTERY)
What **internal barriers** to making this investment do you believe your students may have? (Use the *Resistance Analysis Worksheet* on page 82 to identify specific internal barriers.)	Barrier #1: I've identified some students who don't think that the homework is really meaningful and can't see how it will help them. Barrier #2: Other students have trouble following through with homework tasks. When they encounter difficulty or become confused, they just give up.

How will you address these reasons for resisting? (Use the *Resistance Analysis Worksheet* on page 82 to identify possible solutions.)	For Barrier #1: The root cause is a lack of relevance. I need to do a better job connecting homework with practice and help students see the importance of practice. I've been grading the homework each day, but that isn't really helping. I should have students set weekly goals and then have them do drills to track their speed and accuracy completing the problems so that they can see how the homework practice is helping them. For Barrier #2: The root cause is a fear of failure: I think the "break glass" strategies I put in place will help students persist when they hit a wall. I also think that the practice drills and tracking their progress will help students overcome their fear of failure.
How will you phrase your commitment request and help students invest successfully? (Use the *Investment Request and Planning Worksheet* on page 91 to identify how you will ask for and help students commit to investing in your classroom.)	I will start by explaining why homework is important. Then I will ask students to commit to completing their homework each night according to the following guidelines: • Follow directions. • Follow all the steps in the process. • Show all work. • Attempt all problems. • Submit by the due date. • Ask for help if you get stuck. Next, I will set up a drill each day where students use the skills they have practiced for homework and track their progress in speed and accuracy in completing their problems. Students will keep a chart, set goals for speed and accuracy each week, and chart their homework completion and success on a corresponding chart. We will discuss how homework is helping their progress and adjust their homework assignments as needed to give them more choice and autonomy to choose those assignments that will give them more mastery.

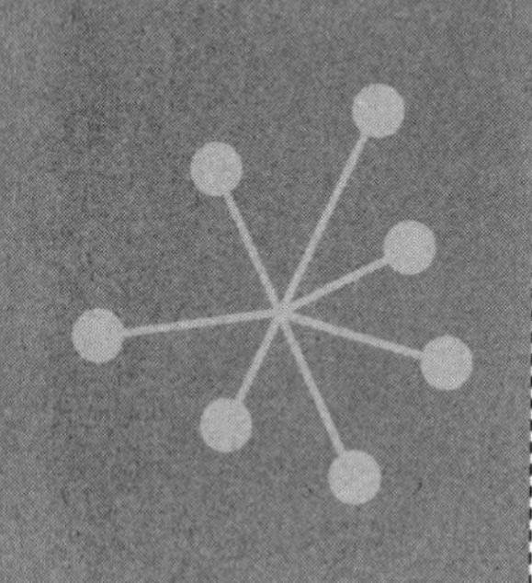

References

Csikszentmihalyi, M., Abuhamdeh, S., & Nakamura, J. (2005). Flow. In A. Elliot & C. Dweck (Eds.), *Handbook of competence and motivation* (pp. 598–608). New York: Guilford Press.

Deci, E. L., & Moller, A. C. (2005). The concept of competence: A starting place for understanding intrinsic motivation and self-determined extrinsic motivation. In A. Elliot & C. Dweck (Eds.), *Handbook of competence and motivation* (pp. 579–597). New York: Guilford Press.

Dweck, C. S. (2006). *Mindset: The new psychology of success.* New York: Random House.

Gee, J. P. (2007). *What video games have to teach us about learning and literacy.* New York: Palgrave MacMillan.

Harris, J. R. (1998). *The nurture assumption: Why children turn out the way they do.* New York: Simon and Schuster.

Hattie, J. (2009). *Visible learning: A synthesis of over 800 meta-analyses relating to achievement.* London: Routledge.

Heath, C., & Heath, D. (2010). *Switch: How to change things when change is hard.* New York: Broadway Books.

March, J. (1994). *A primer on decision making: How decisions happen.* New York: Free Press.

Marzano, R. (2003). *What works in schools: Translating research into action.* Alexandria, VA: ASCD.

Maslow, A. H. (1943). A theory of human motivation. *Psychological Review, 50,* 370–396.

Parker, L. E., & Lepper, M. R. (1992). Effects of fantasy contexts on children's learning and motivation: Making learning more fun. *Journal of Personality and Social Psychology, 62*(4), 625–633.

Pink, D. (2009). *Drive: The surprising truth about what motivates us.* New York: Riverhead Books.

Saphier, J., & Gower, R. (1997). *The skillful teacher: Building your teaching skills* (5th ed.). Acton, MA: Research for Better Teaching.

Schwartz, B. (2000, January). Self-determination: The tyranny of freedom. *American Psychologist, 55*(1), 79–88.

Sullo, B. (2009). *The motivated student: Unlocking the enthusiasm for learning*. Alexandria, VA: ASCD.

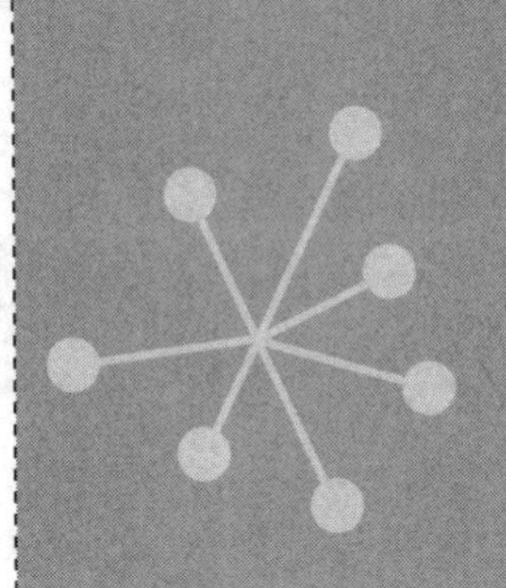

About the Author

Robyn R. Jackson, PhD, is a former high school teacher and middle school administrator. She is currently the President and Founder of Mindsteps Inc., a professional development firm for teachers and administrators that provides workshops and materials designed to help any teacher reach every student. Dr. Jackson is the author of *Never Work Harder Than Your Students and Other Principles of Great Teaching*, *The Differentiation Workbook*, and *The Instructional Leader's Guide to Strategic Conversations with Teachers* as well as the how-to guides in the **Mastering the Principles of Great Teaching** series. You can sign up for Dr. Jackson's monthly e-newsletter at www.mindstepsinc.com, follow Dr. Jackson on Twitter at @robyn_mindsteps, or reach her via e-mail at robyn@mindstepsinc.com.

Want More?

Additional resources are available on this book's companion website at www.mindstepsinc.com/motivation. There, you can

- Download copies of the worksheets in this book.
- Find and link to additional free resources.
- Download related video content that provides additional explanations.
- Post your own comments and hear what other readers are saying.
- Sign up to receive a free monthly e-newsletter.
- Explore lots of other reader-only content.

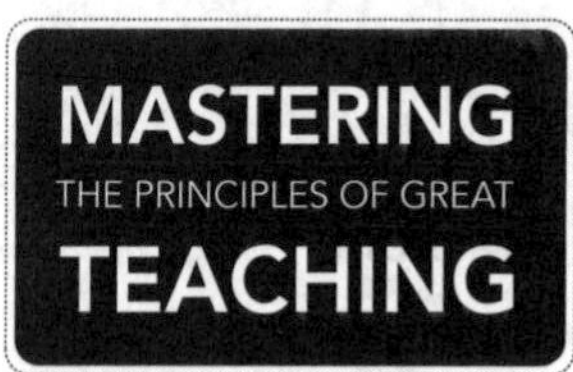

Watch for other books in this series, coming soon.

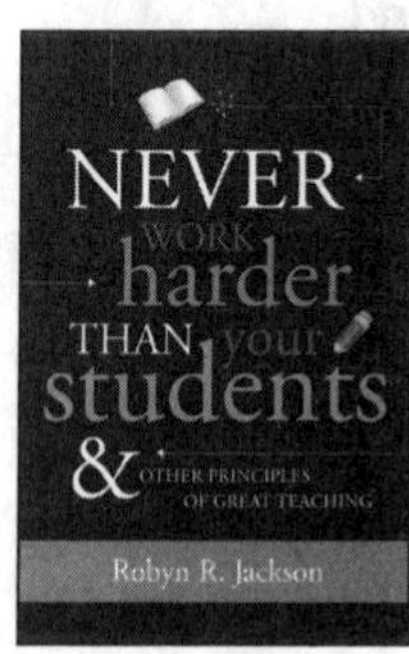

Much more about master teachers can be found in this series' companion book, *Never Work Harder Than Your Students and Other Principles of Great Teaching* by Robyn R. Jackson (#109001).